Your journey to becoming a comic artist has begun. You will absolutely enjoy this easy 4-step instruction book and be well on your way to becoming a drawing genius. So grab your paper and pencil and let's get started!!!

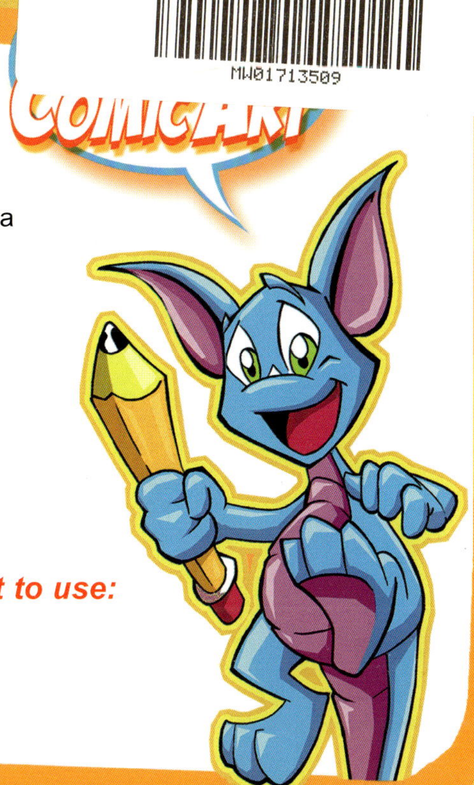

***Things you will need:***

- Pencil
- Eraser
- Paper
- Black ink pen

***Things you may want to use:***

- Scrap paper
- Pencil crayons
- Markers

***Remember to press lightly when drawing, to make your extra lines easier to erase when you are finished.***

## STEP 1: LAYOUT OF YOUR CHARACTERS

First lightly draw or trace the outlines of these characters. Start by drawing the blue lines and then add in the red lines. This will give you the basic outline of your characters.

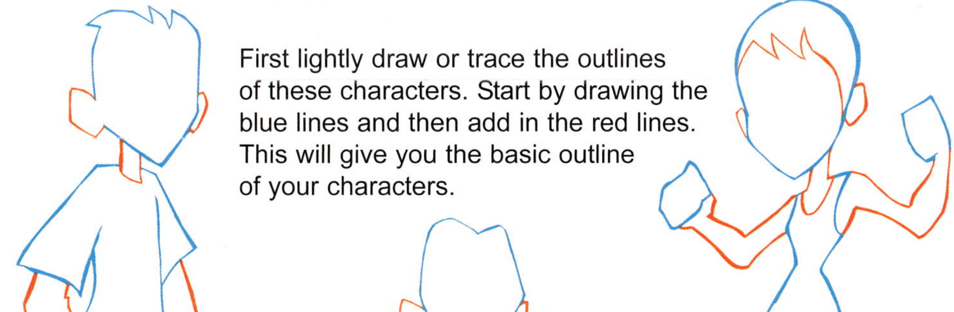

## STEP 2: DEFINING YOUR CHARACTERS

Now draw what you see in red. These lines will help to define your characters, such as the face, hair, fingers, etc.

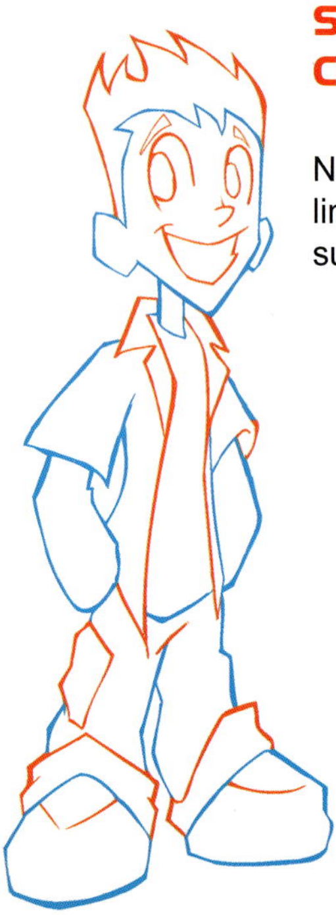

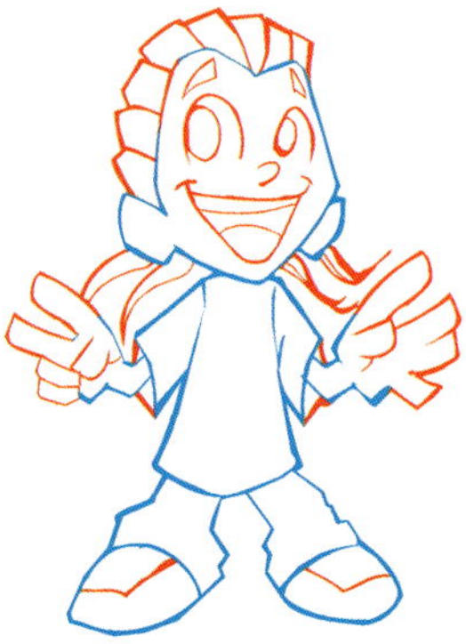

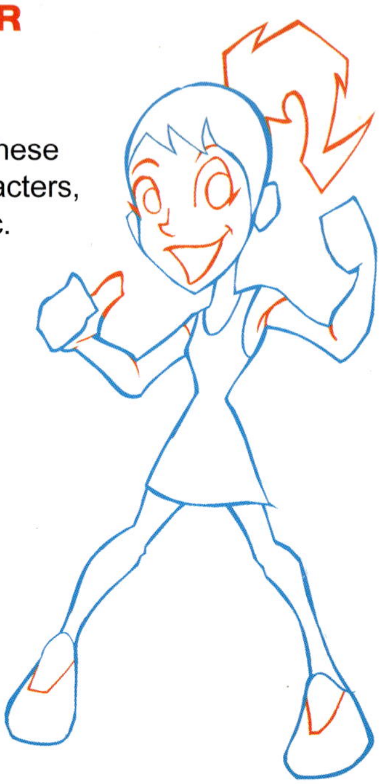

## STEP 3: DETAILING YOUR CHARACTERS

Now that you have finished the bigger details for your characters, you are going to add in the smaller details. Draw what you see here in red.

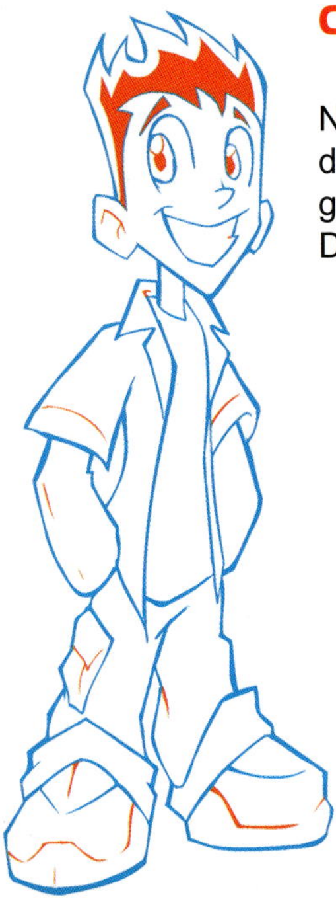

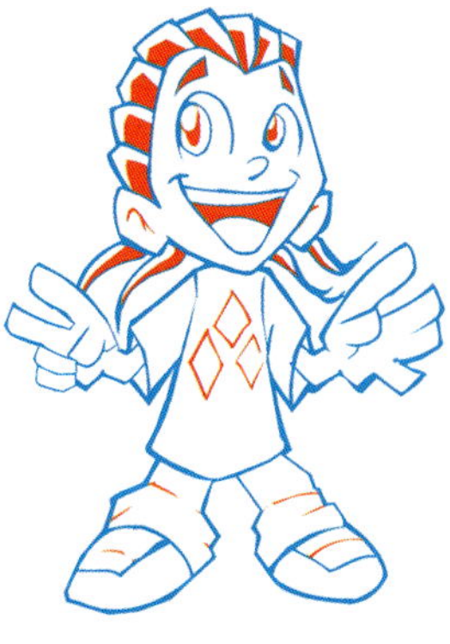

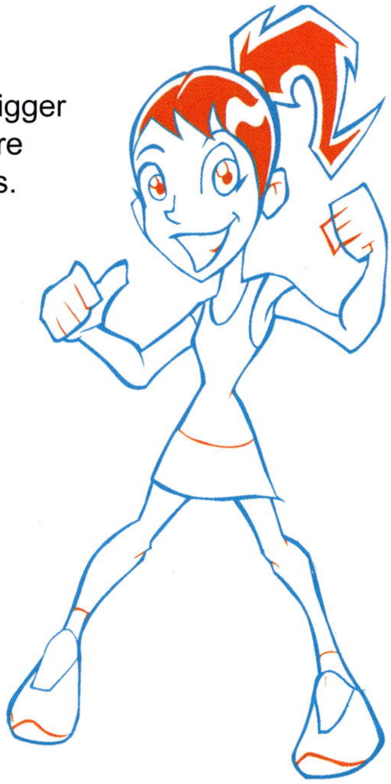

## STEP 4: INKING YOUR CHARACTERS

After you're finished drawing your characters, using a black ink pen trace over the lines that you need, and erase any extra lines.

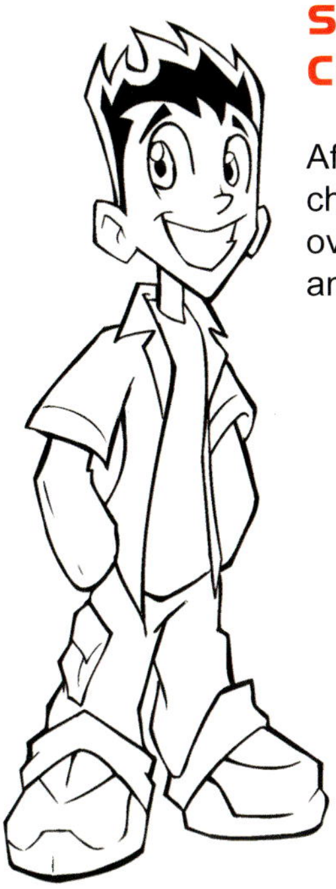
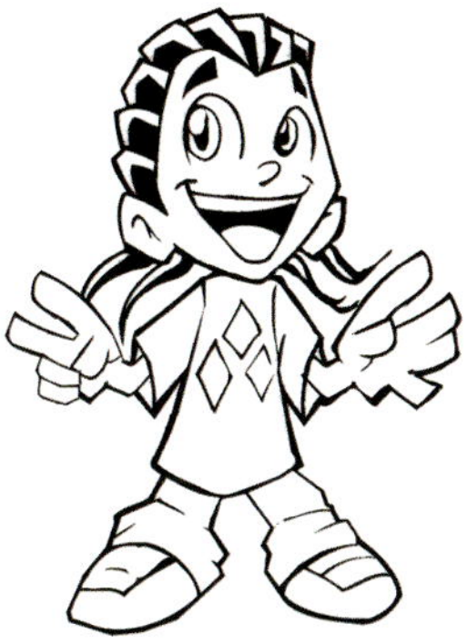
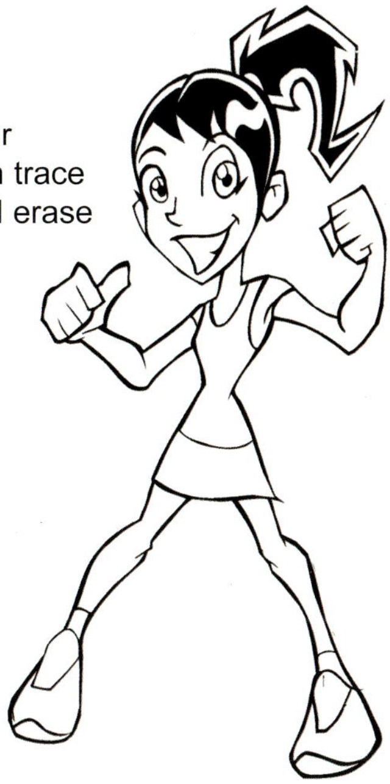

*Use these 4 steps while drawing all the characters in this book.*

## COLORING YOUR CHARACTERS

When coloring your characters start by using the lightest color as your base, and then add darker colors for shading. You can use pencil crayons or markers to color your characters.

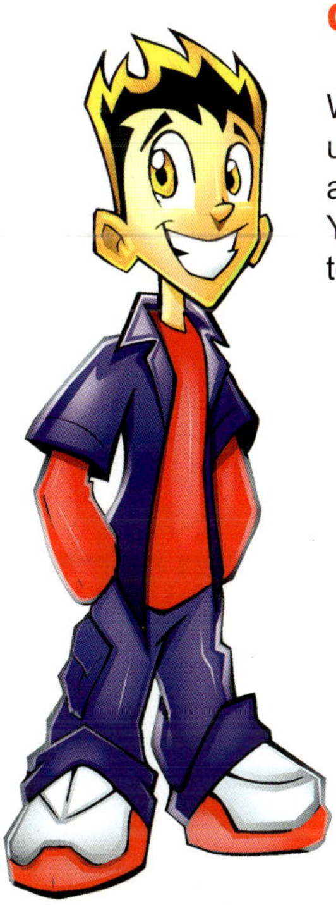
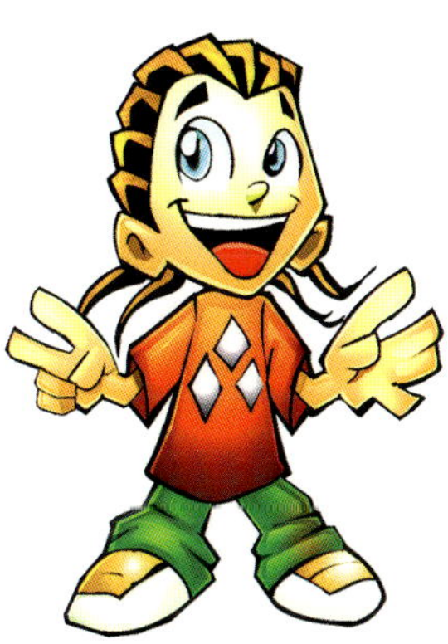
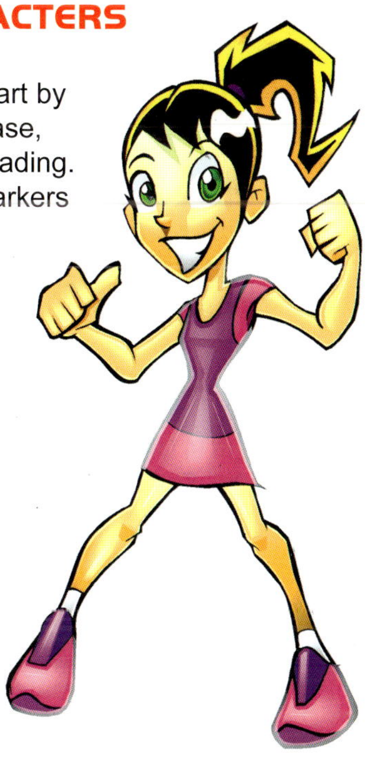

# Cole

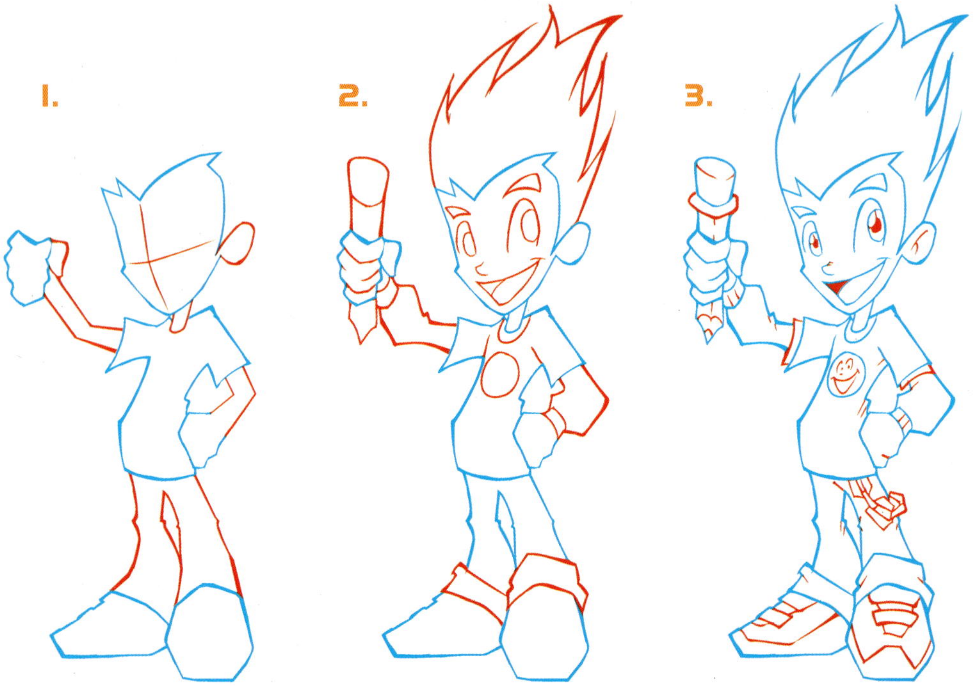


***COLE*** is smart and very outgoing. He loves skateboarding and robots more than anything. Cole has created a robot character named ***Ultra Boy***.

Follow these steps to draw Cole.

4.

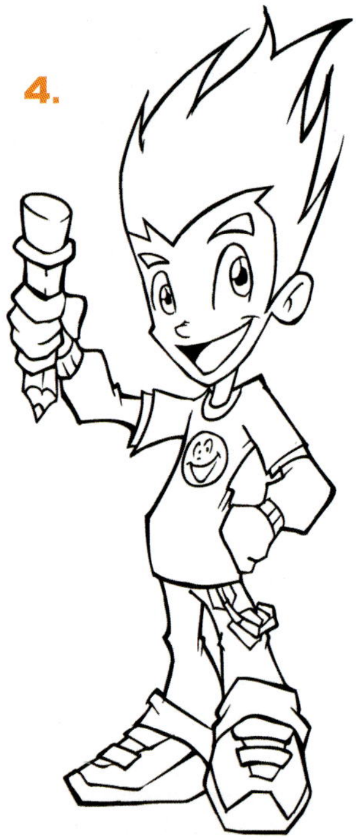

Now help Cole draw Ultra Boy.

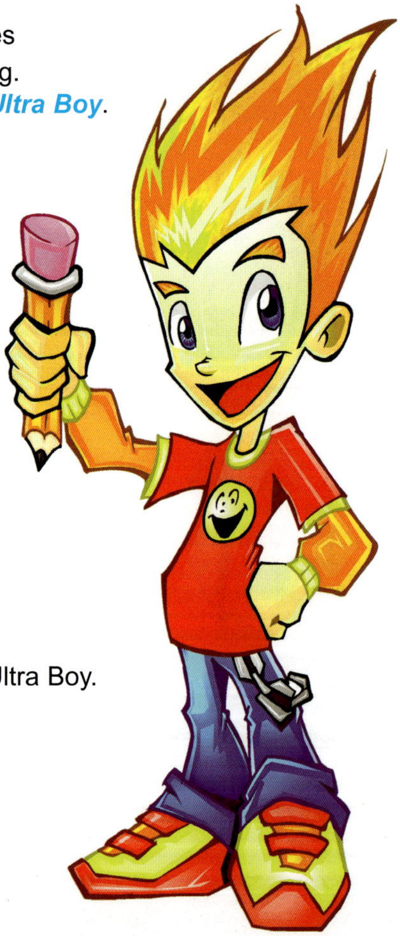

# ULTRA BOY

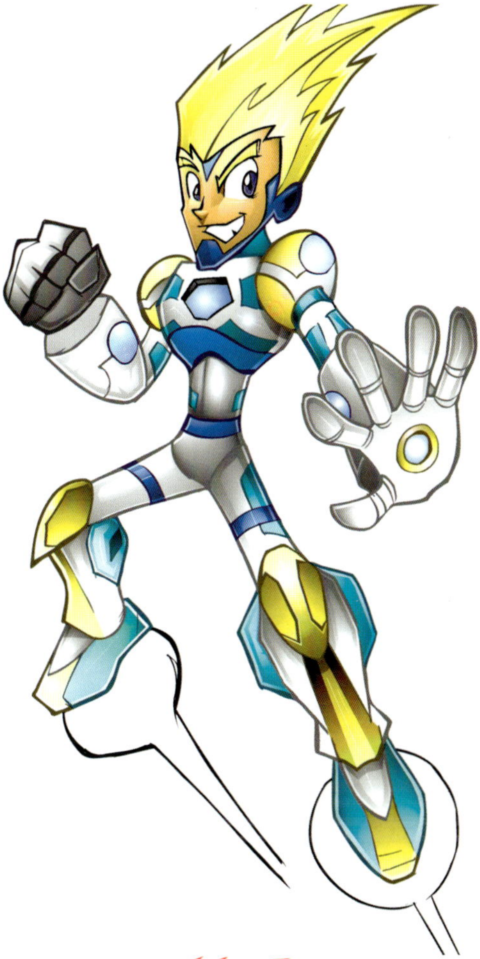

1.

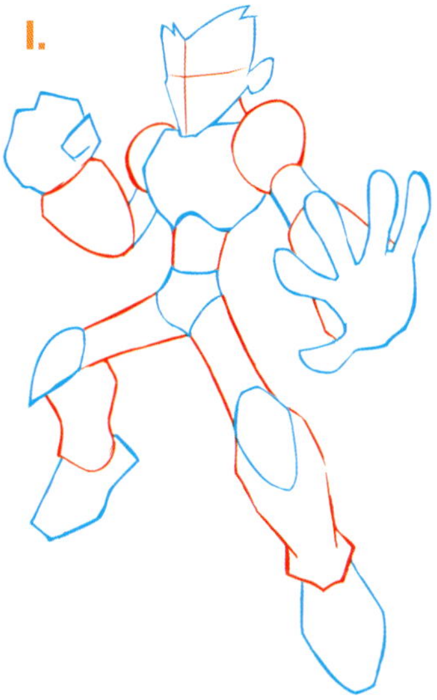

**ULTRA BOY** is a futuristic character, who gets his energy from the sun. He has unlimited endurance and strength, and can fly at super speeds.

2.

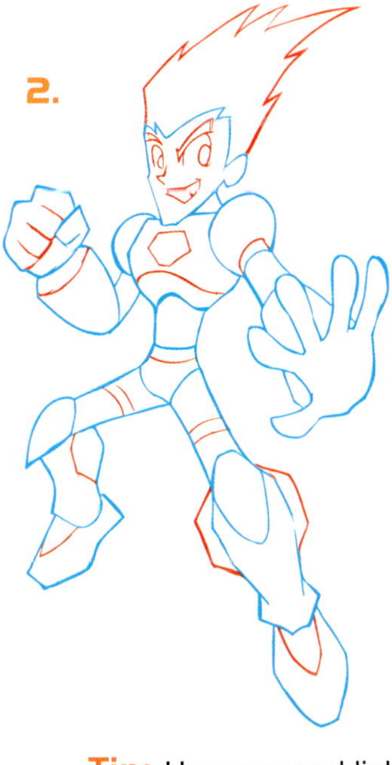

3.

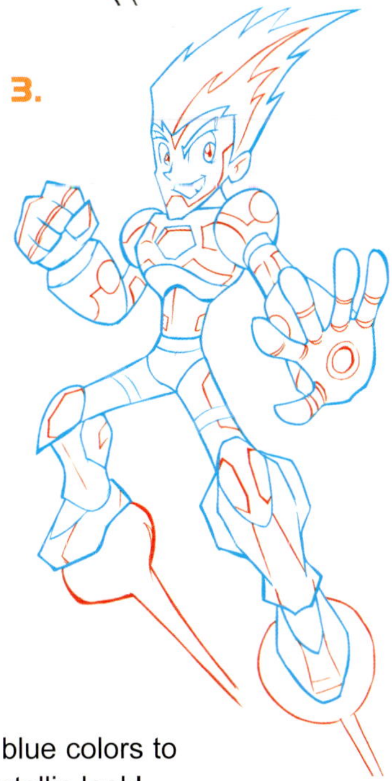

4.

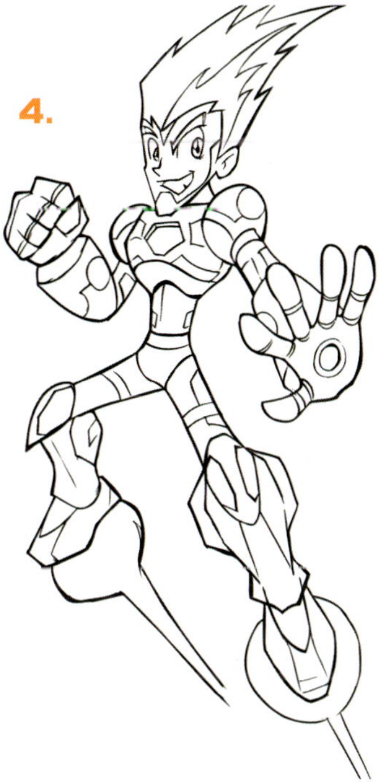

**Tip:** Use gray and light blue colors to give Ultra Boy a more metallic look!

# Tavon

1.

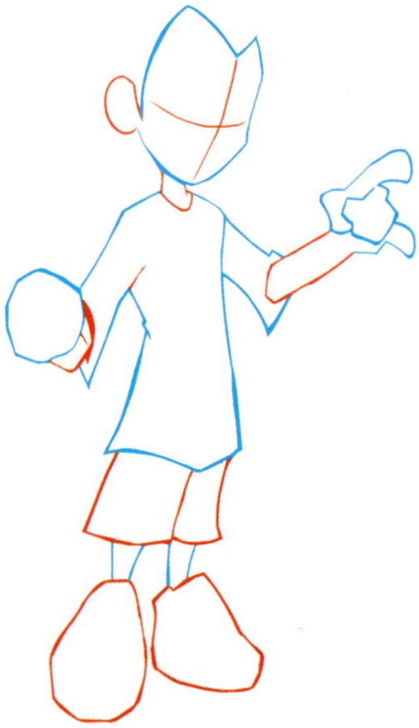

***TAVON*** is the star of his basketball team. He really likes to play sports and he has a lot of friends. He's always wanted to be able to go back in time or skip ahead to see what he'll be doing in the future. So, Tavon's designed a character that can do just that, his name is ***Atomic Jolt.***

2.

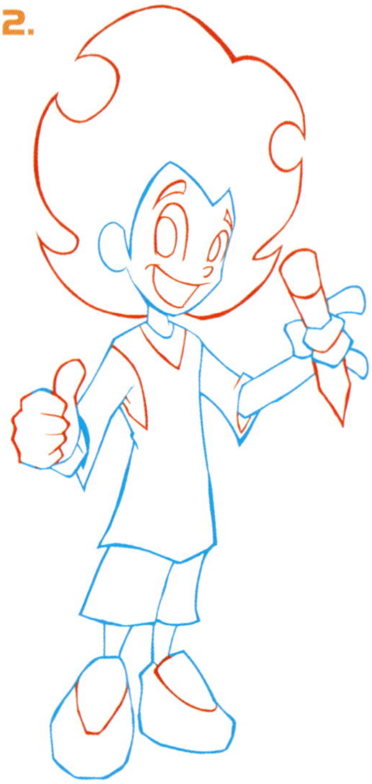

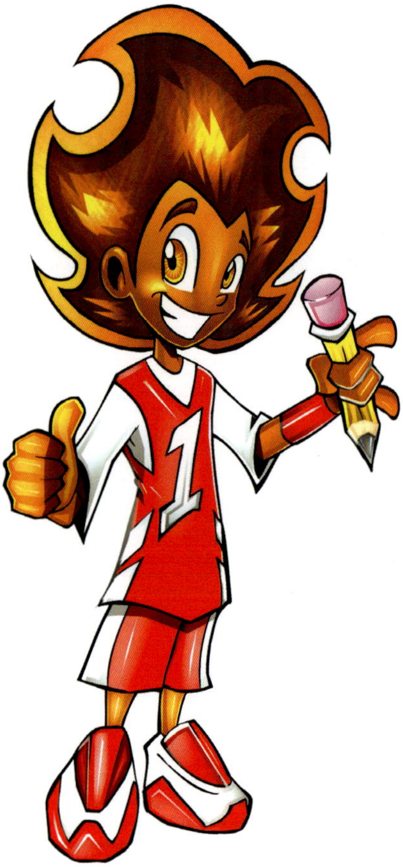

3.

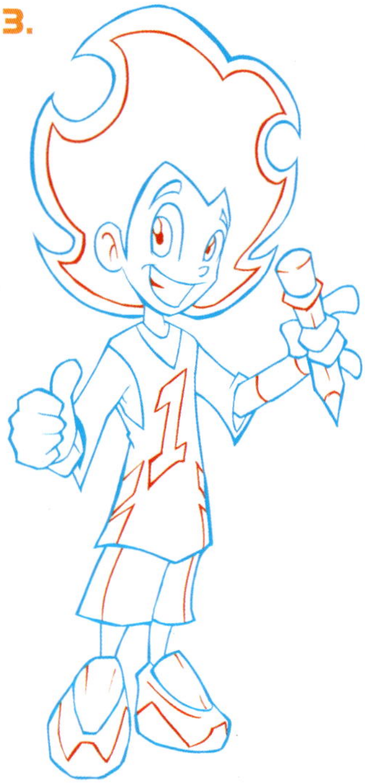

4.

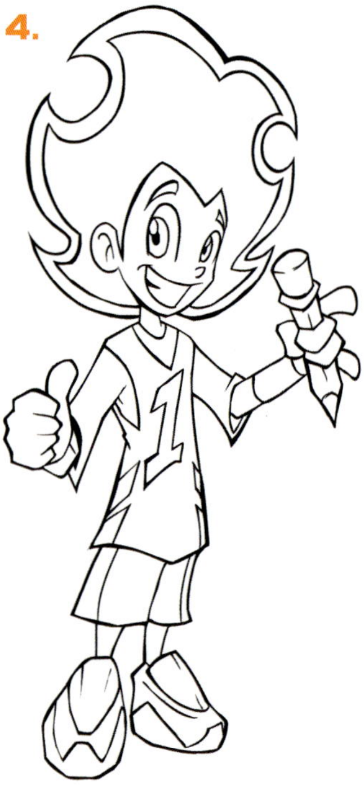

# Atomic Jolt

**ATOMIC JOLT** is as fast as lightning. He wears a supercharged costume that helps him travel through time. He can absorb and store energy, and when in battle, he can release an electric blast from his hands.

1.

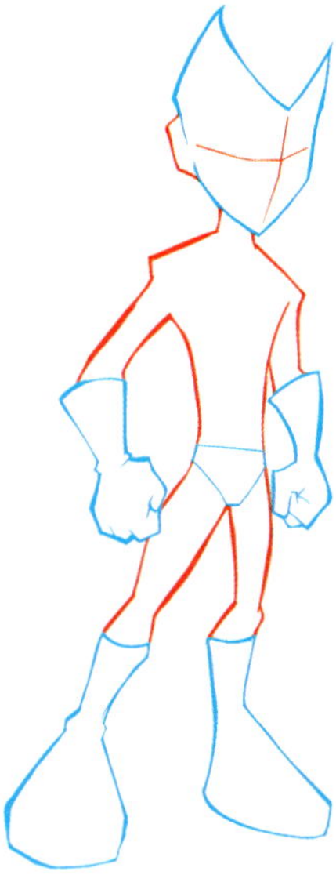

2.

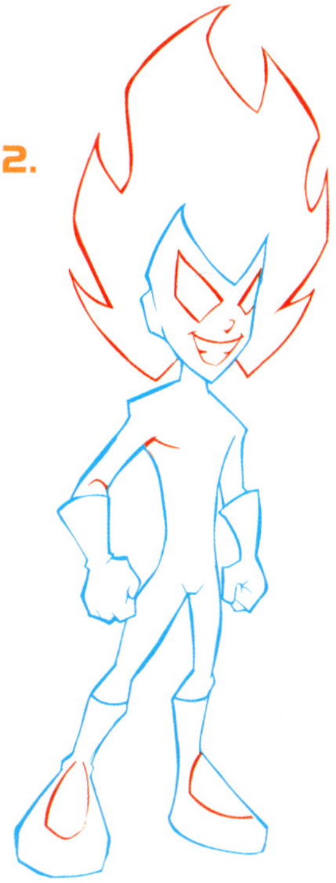

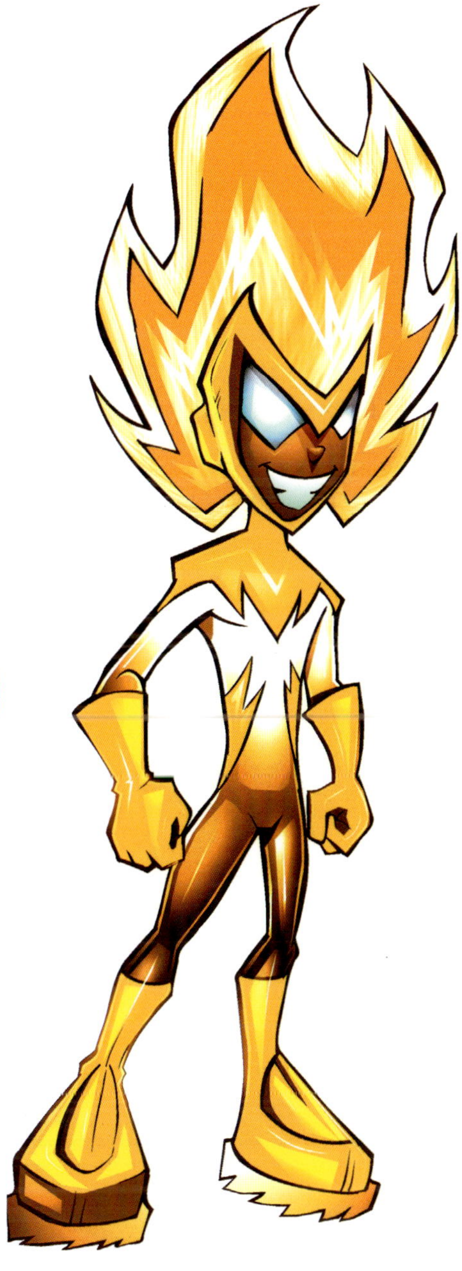

3.

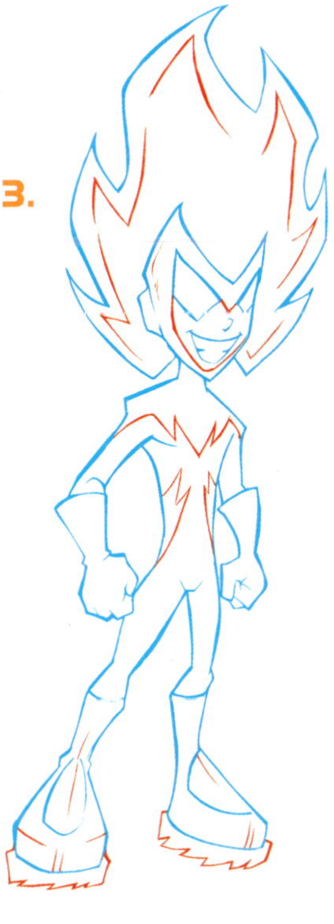

4.

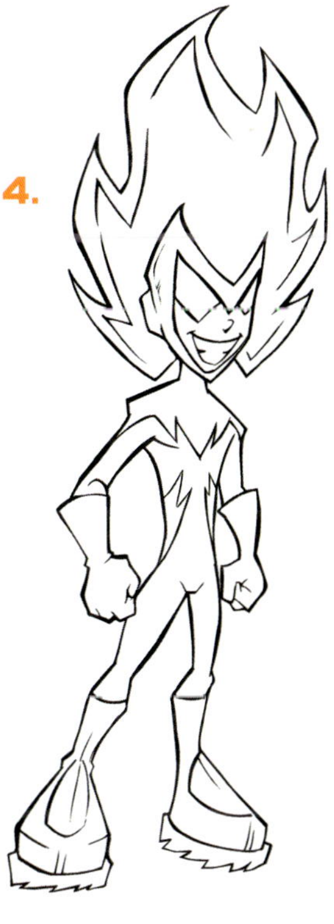

# Zoey

1.

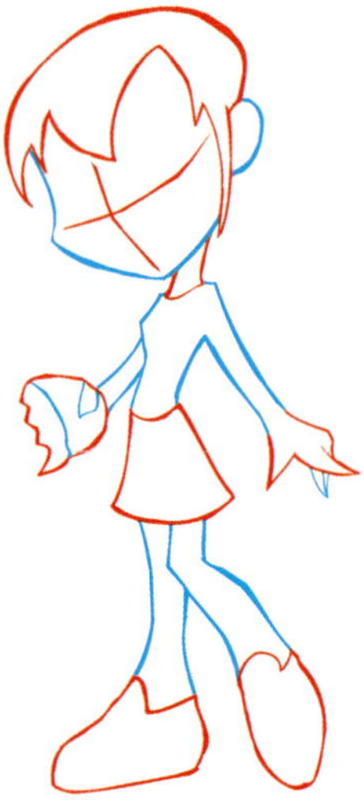

2.

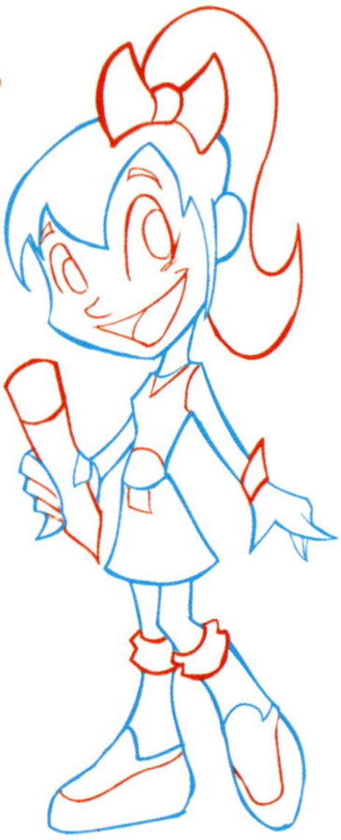

3.

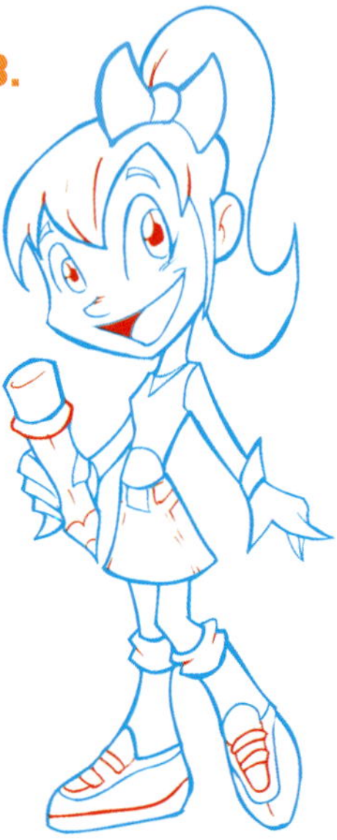

***ZOEY*** is a trendy girl, who really likes to shop and hang out with her friends. She is an awesome gymnast and ballerina. She's always liked fairies and has dreamt of being one herself. She has created a flower fairy named ***Felicia***.

4.

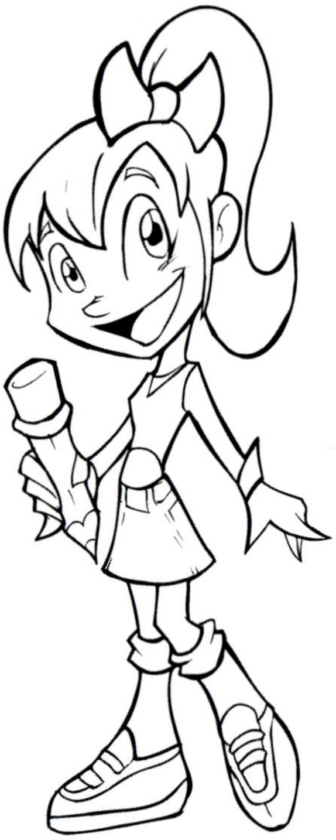

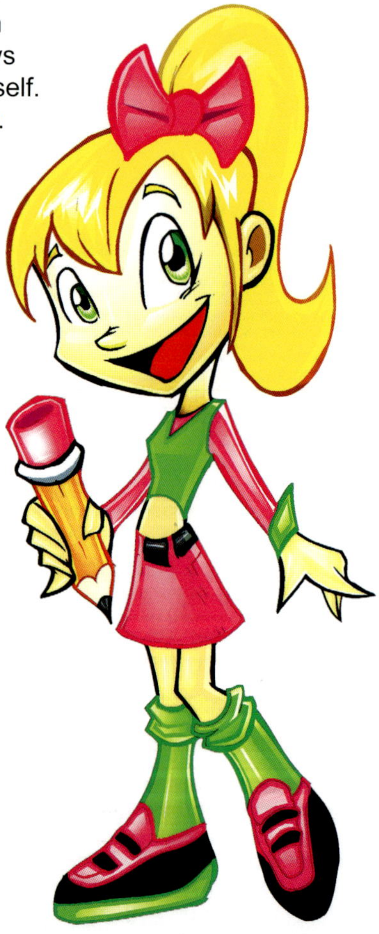

# Felicia

1.

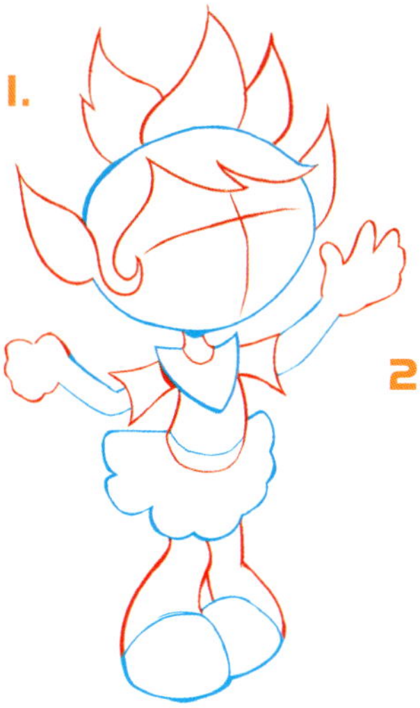

2.

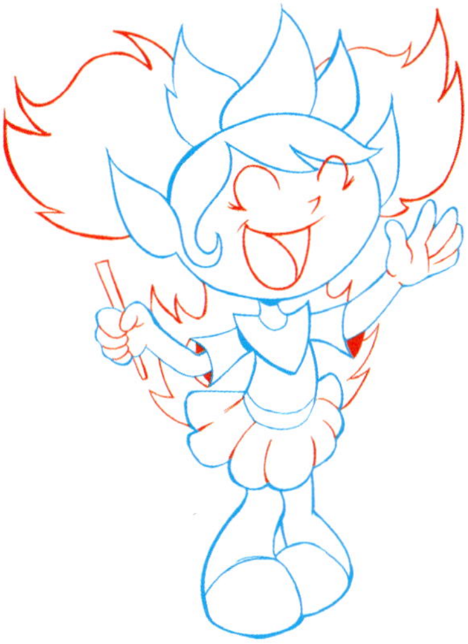

3.

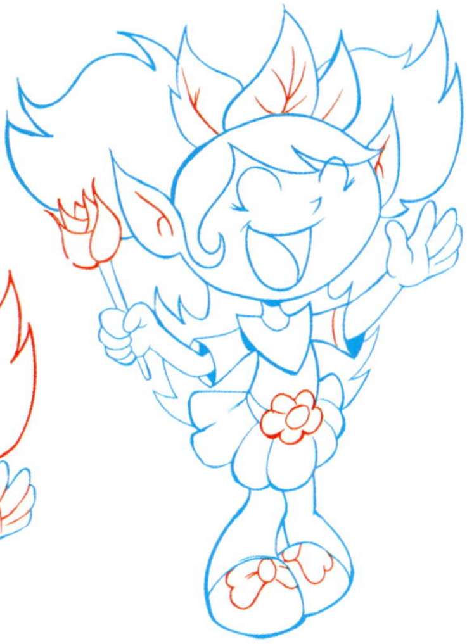

**FELICIA** is a very magical fairy and lives in an enchanted forest. She loves flowers and can make anything she wants look like one. Her wand is a purple rose and she can cast spells, to help people.

4.

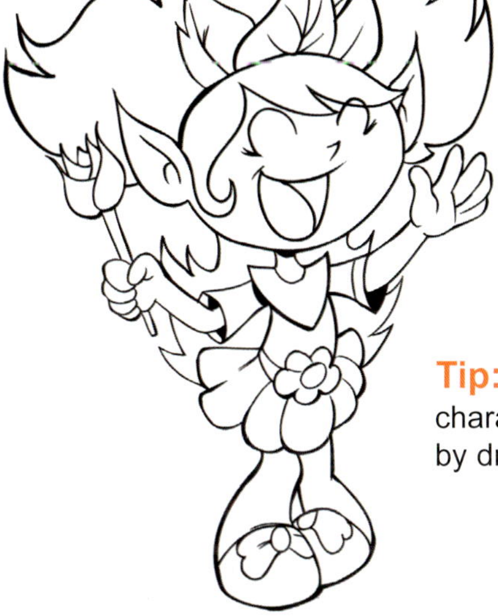

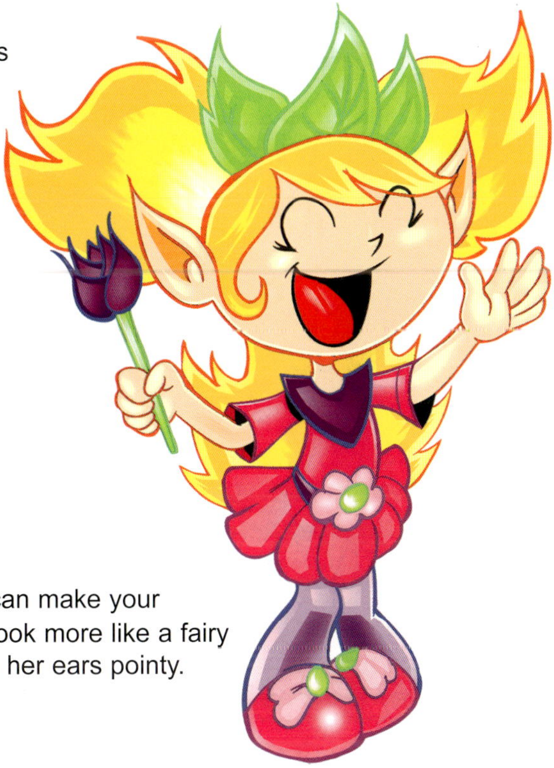

**Tip:** You can make your character look more like a fairy by drawing her ears pointy.

# Keisha

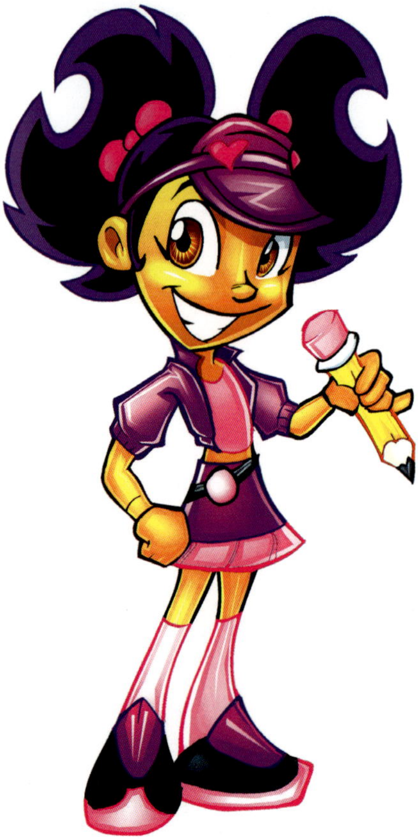

**KEISHA** loves to draw comic characters so much, she has decided to draw herself as one. Follow these steps to draw Keisha, and then try to draw yourself as a character! Would you be a Princess like the character Keisha has created?

1.

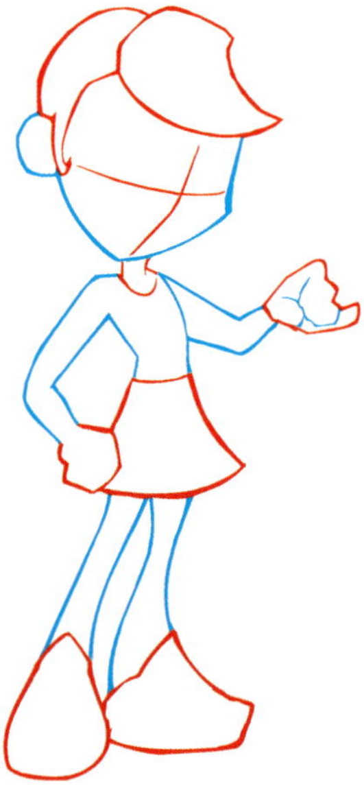

2.

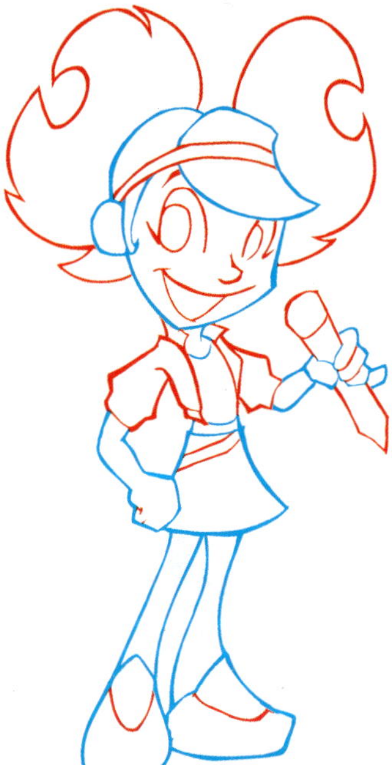

3.

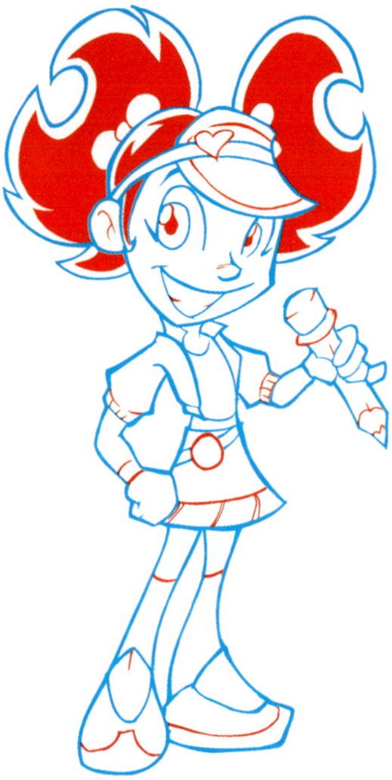

4.

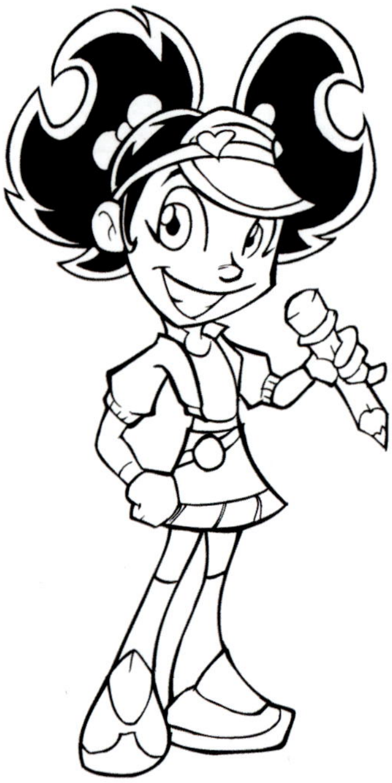

# Princess Skyla

1.

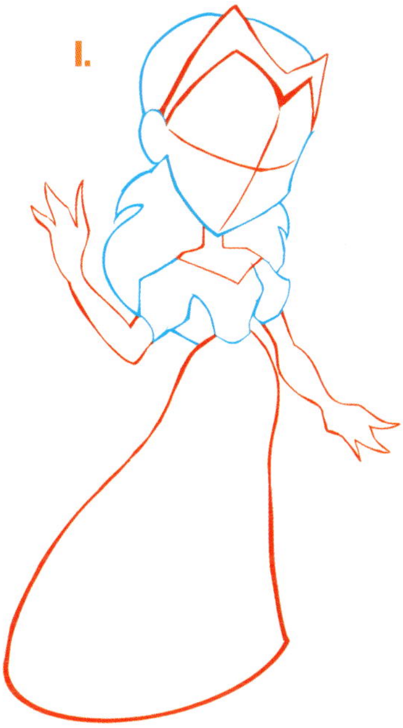

2.

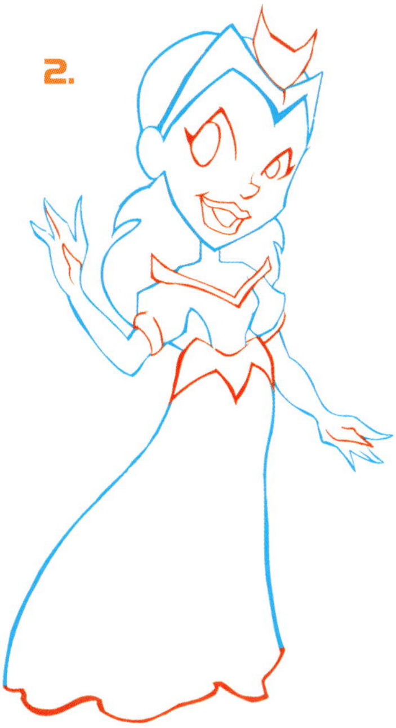

3.

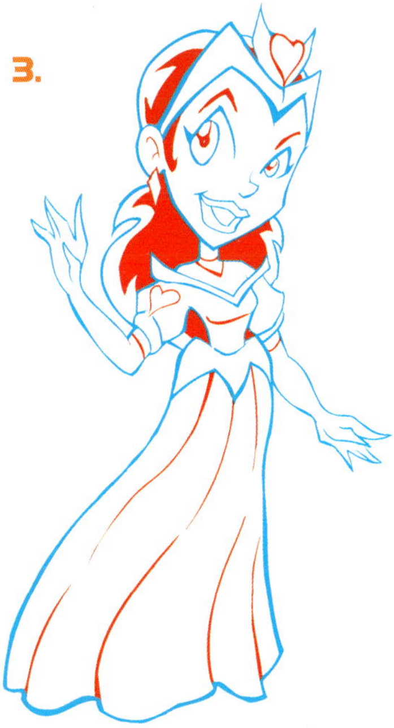

**PRINCESS SKYLA** lives in a far away kingdom. She has magical powers and uses them to make sure everyone is happy! What magical power would you have if you were a character?

4.

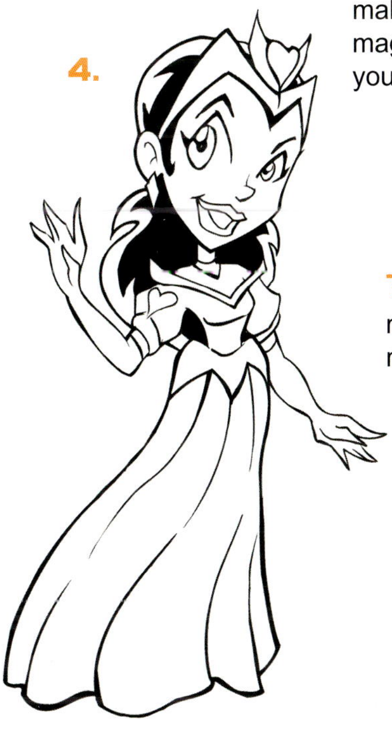

**Tip:** A long dress will make Princess Skyla look more stylish and elegant.

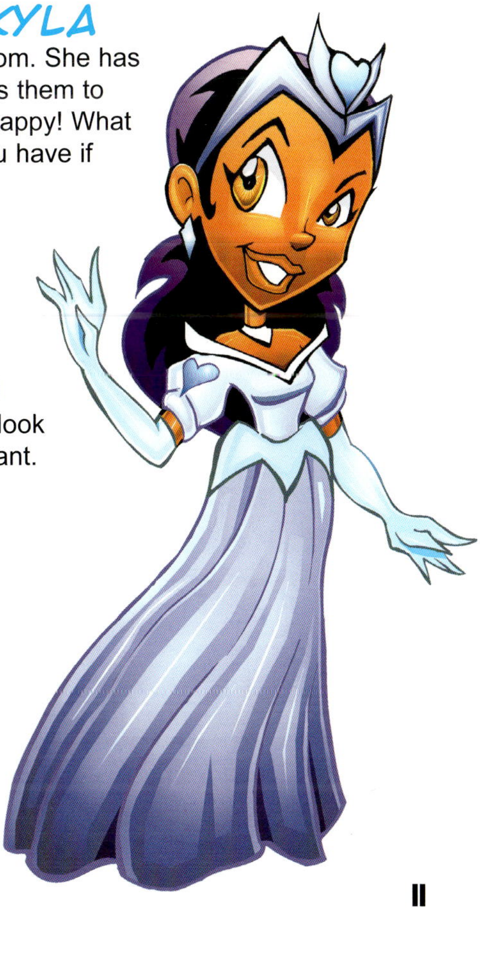

# Tiny, Hanna and Petey

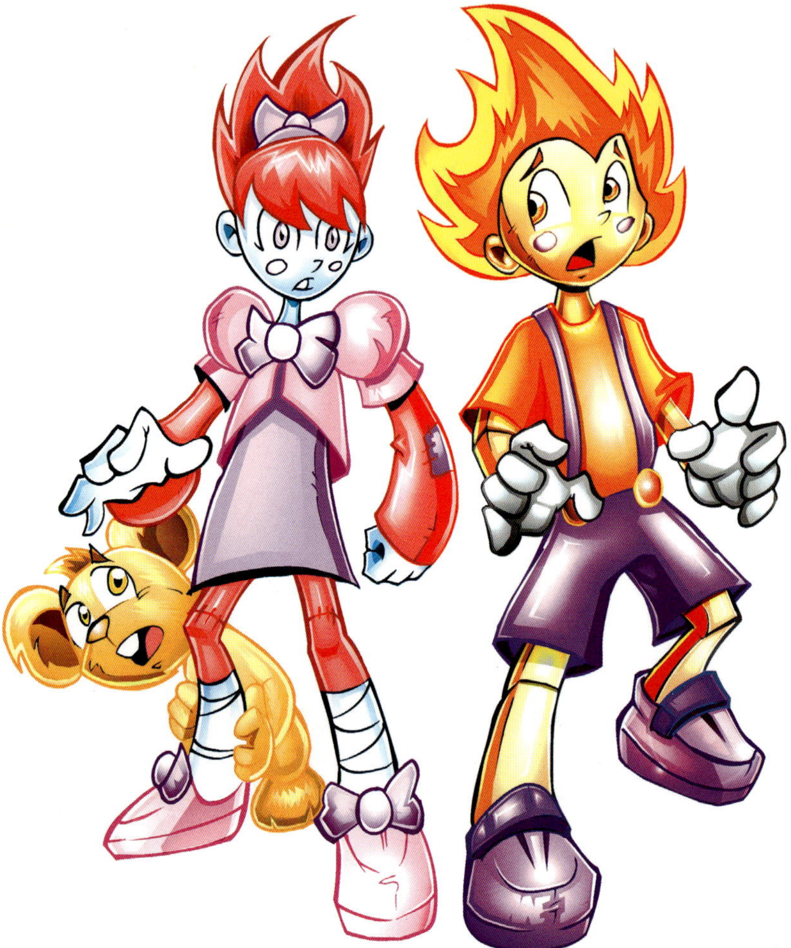

1.

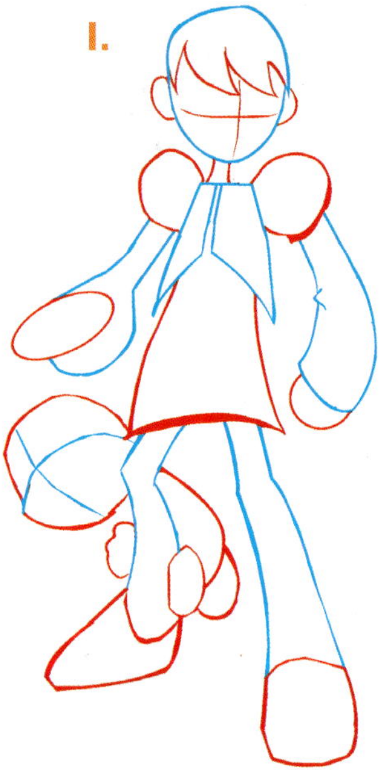

## TINY, HANNA AND PETEY

Have you ever had a toy or stuffed animal that you could not put down or ever wished they would come to life?

Toy characters are very stiff looking almost like they are frozen. By using bright colors you will make your characters look alive on the page.

**Tip:** Adding patches or stitches to the character can make them look more old and ragged.

1.

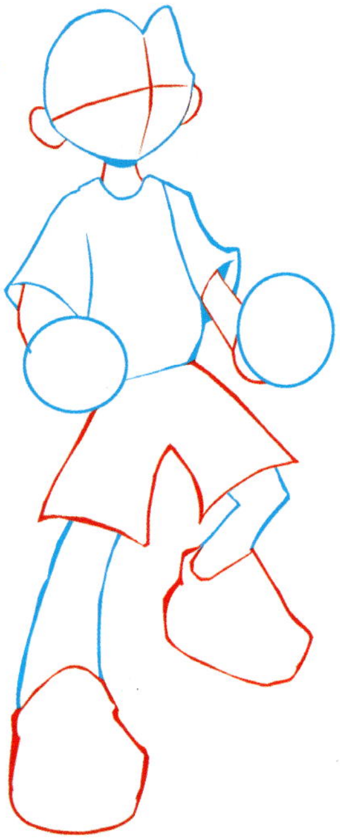

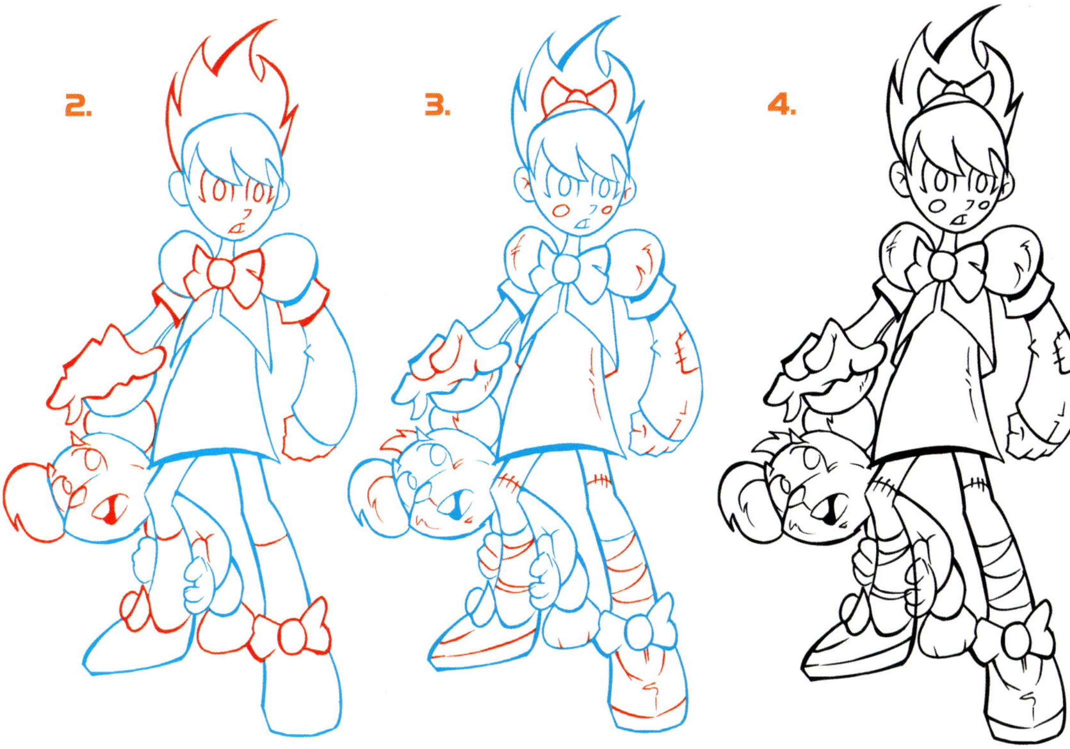


When you're finished your drawings, add lines going to the hands and the feet from the top of the page that look like strings, transforming the toys to look like puppets.

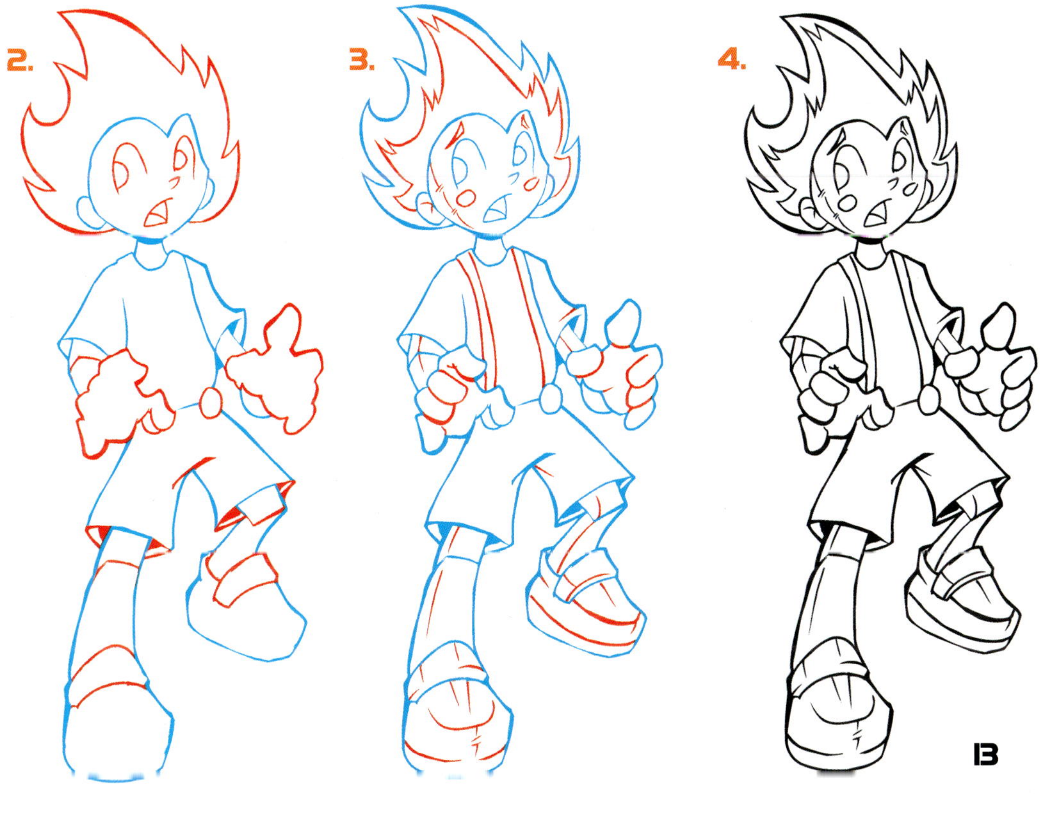

# Little Kylie

1.

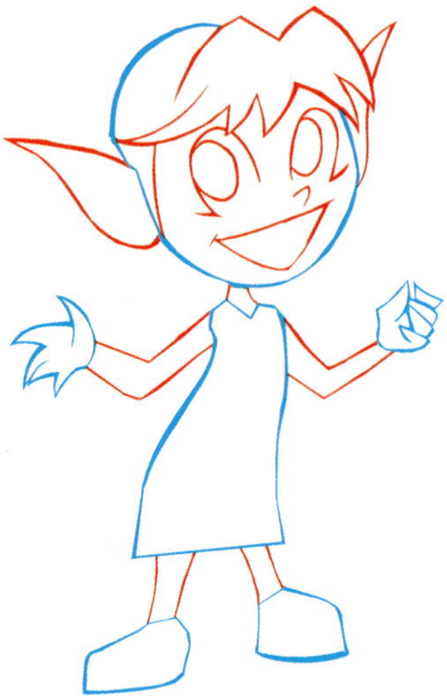

2.

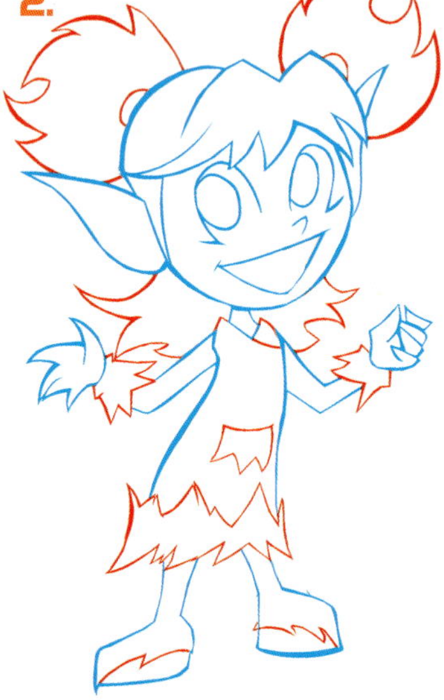

3.

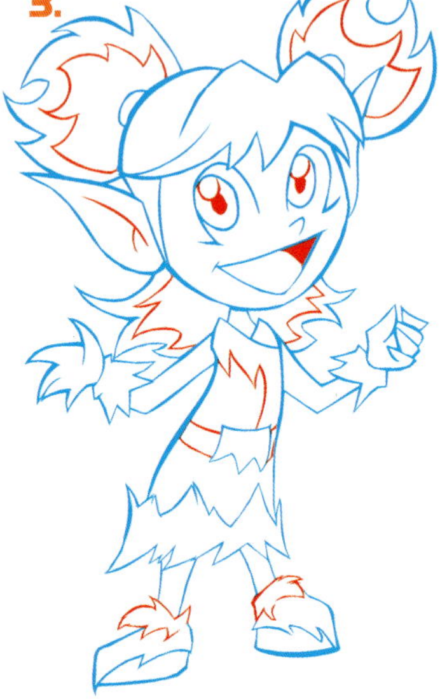

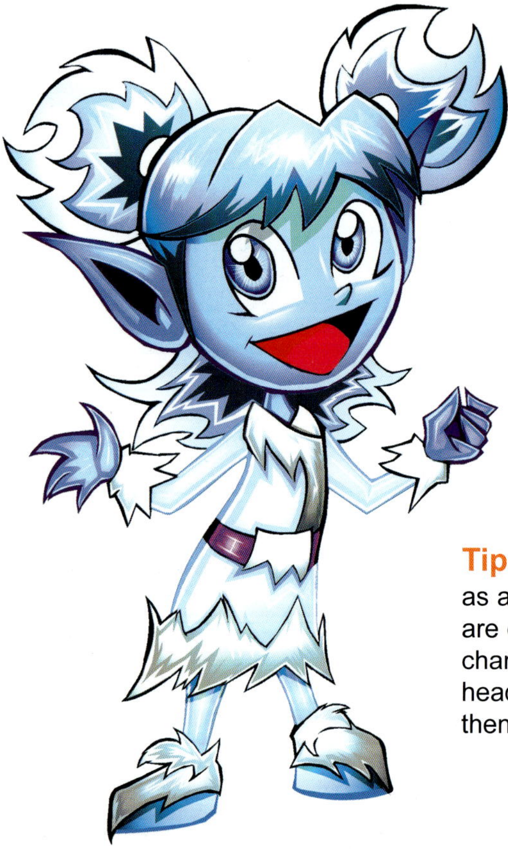

**KYLIE** is super cool. She can freeze anything she wants just by touching it. She's grown into her superpowers and uses them only when she really has too.

4.

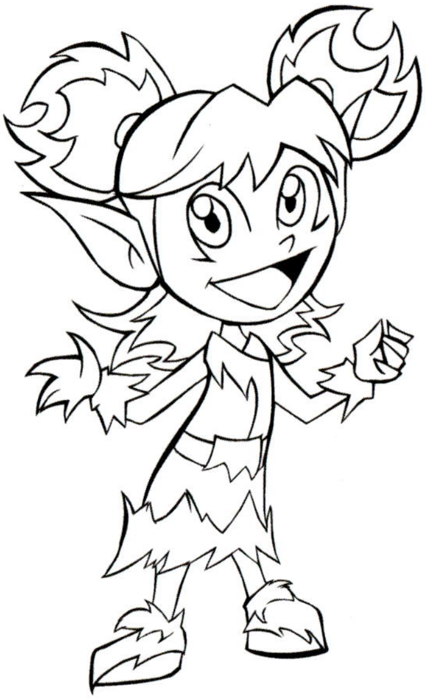

**Tip:** This is Kylie as a kid. When you are drawing younger characters their heads are bigger then their bodies.

# Teen Kylie

1.

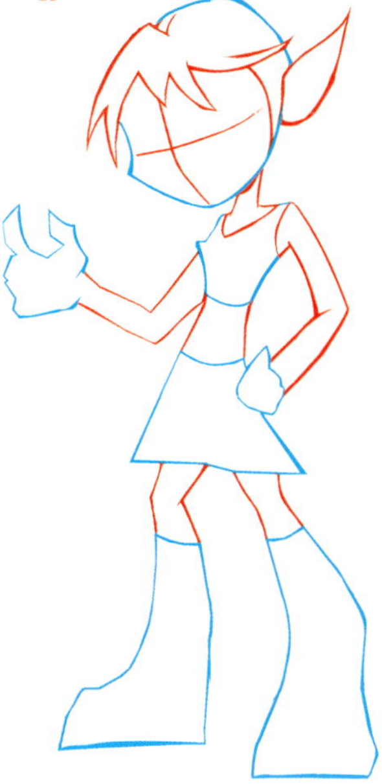

2.

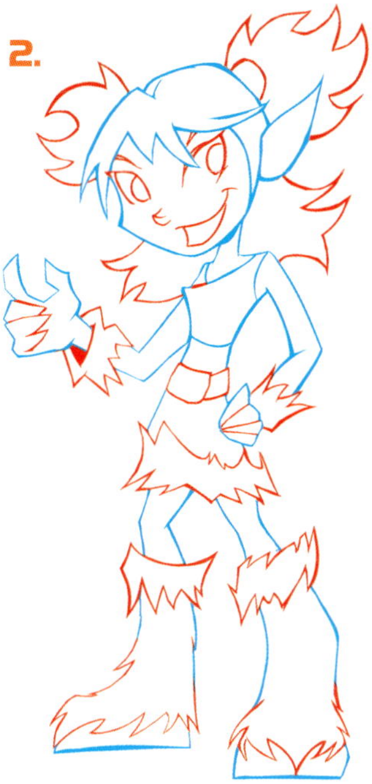

3.

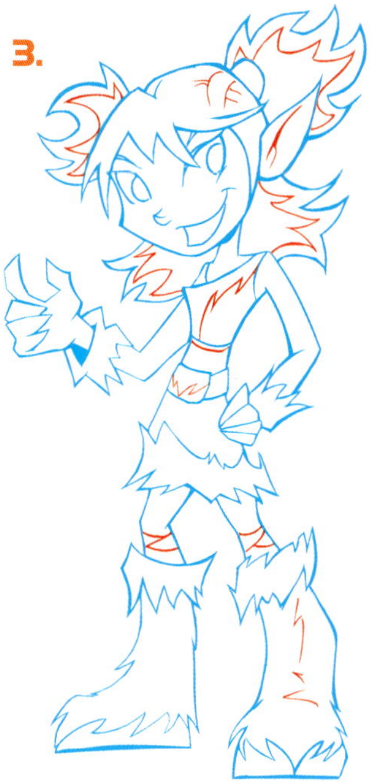

Here's **Kylie** as a teenager. Her head is a bit smaller now but is still a bit bigger then her body is. When drawing your characters from young to old, make sure you keep them looking the same so that people recognize they are the same person.

4.

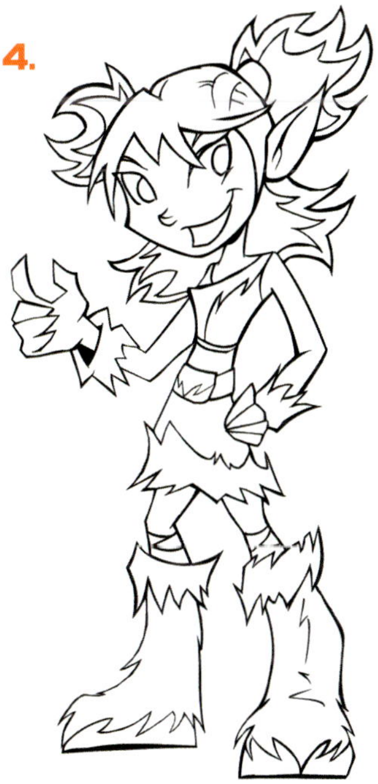

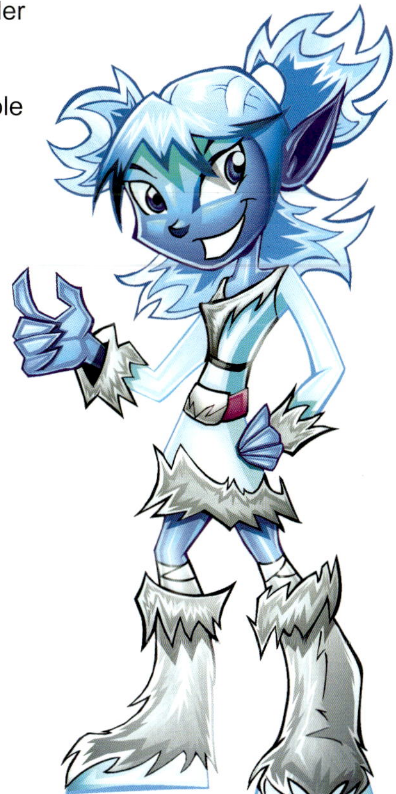

# Knightly

1.

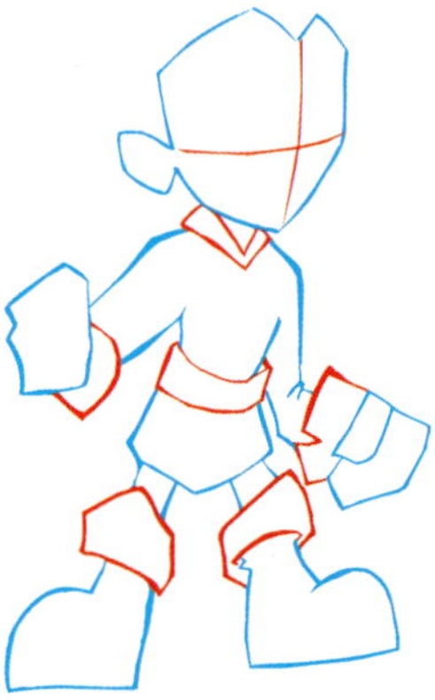

2.

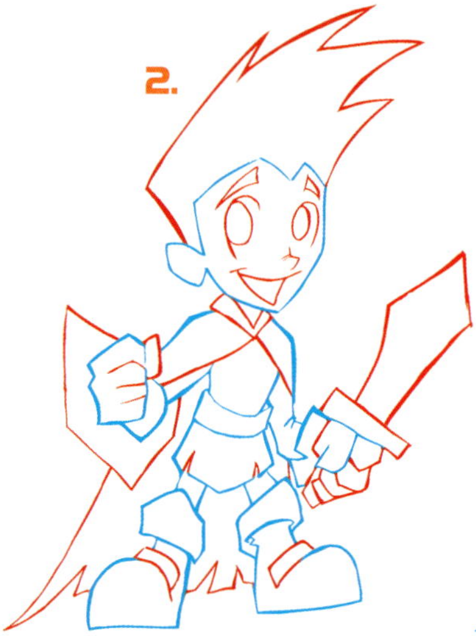

3.

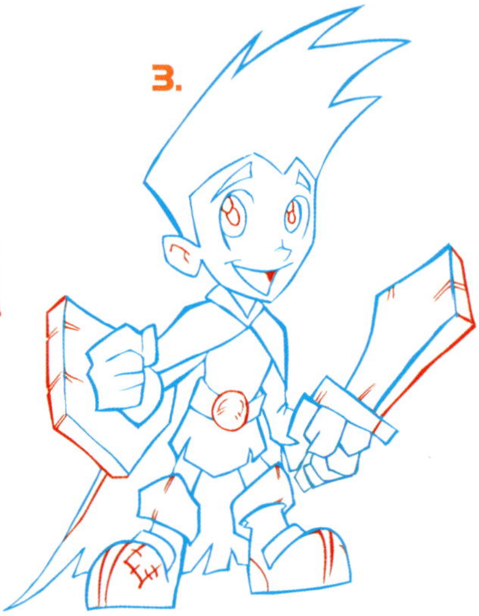

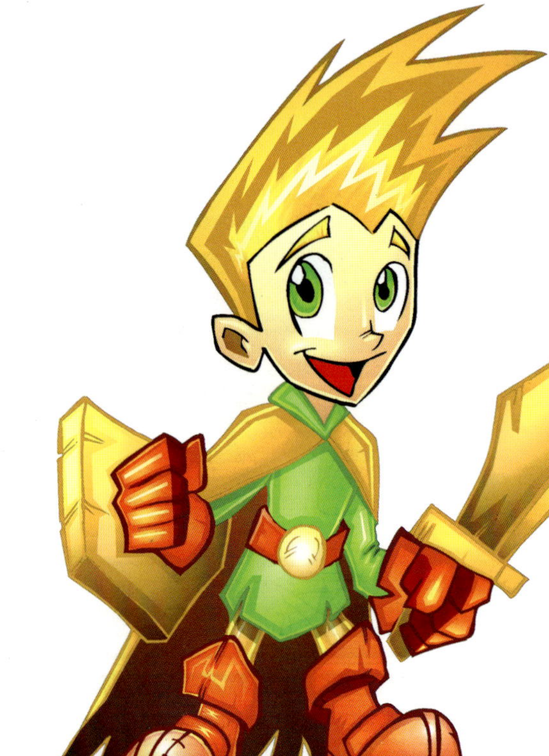

**KNIGHTLY** is a warrior in training, although he is the smallest of his 5 brothers. He believes one day, he will be the most powerful knight in his kingdom.

4.

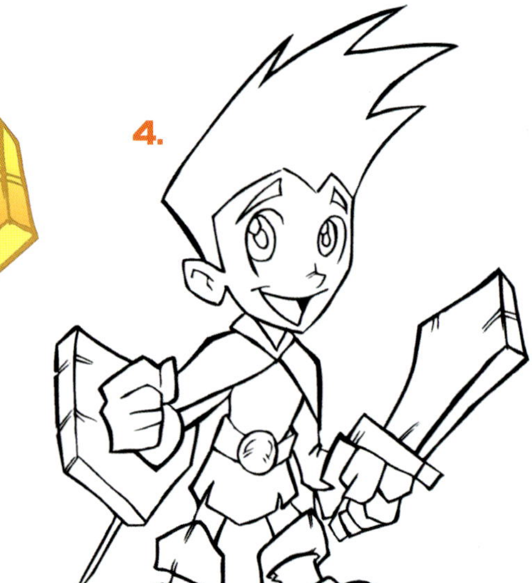

# Knightly

1.

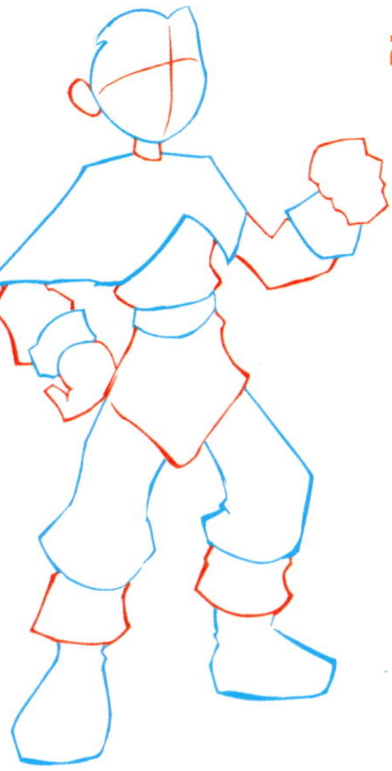

2.

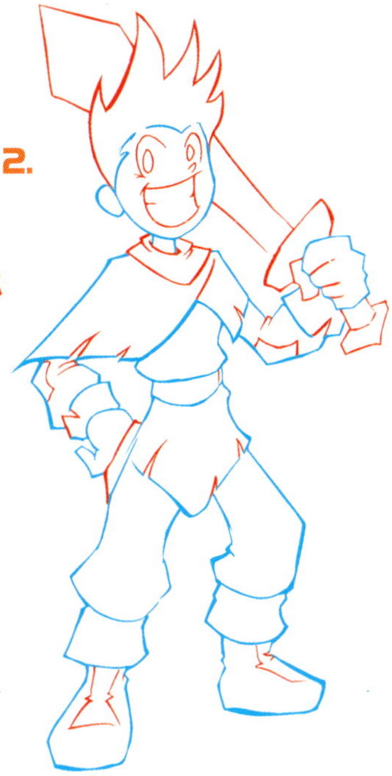

3.

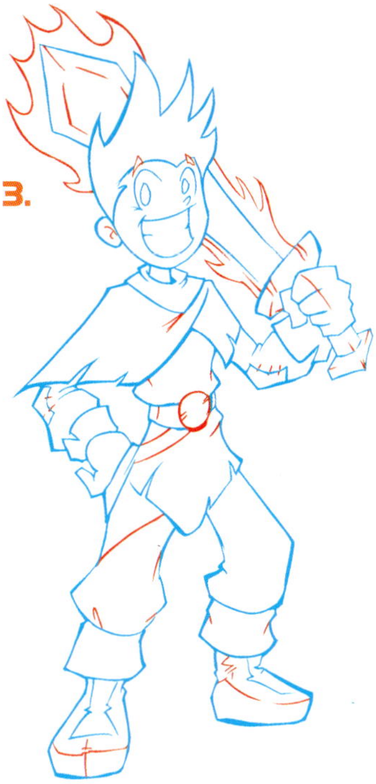

**KNIGHTLY** is a teenager now. After a few years of training, his father believes he is ready to inherit the power of the legendary Sword of Light. Although it will take many more years of training to learn the full power of the sword.

4.

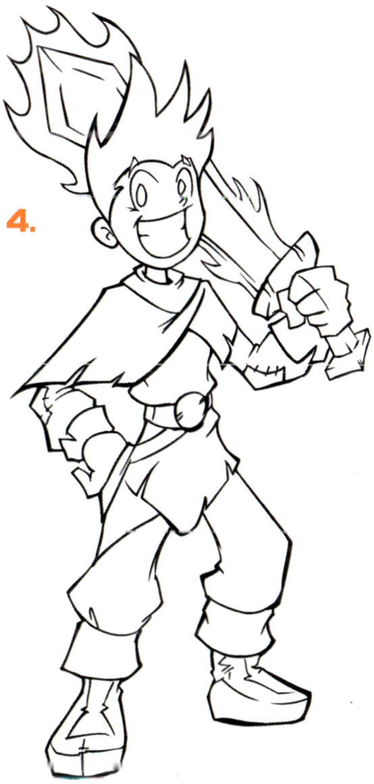

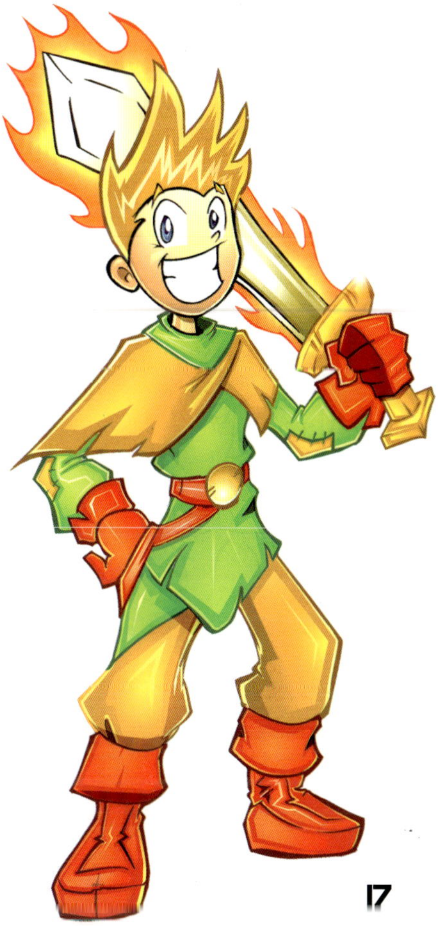

# Kylie

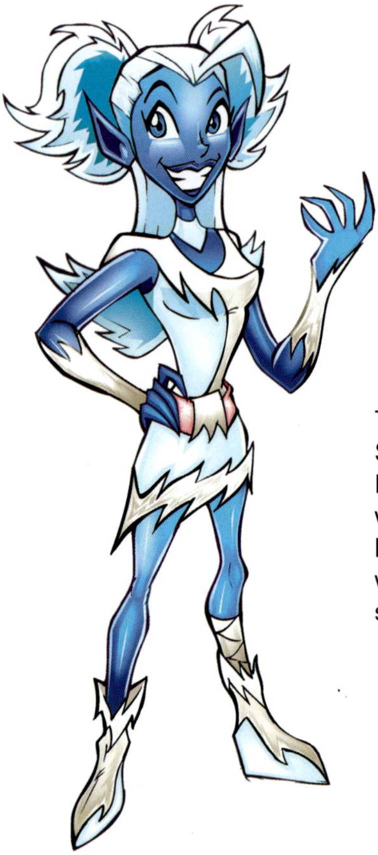

1.

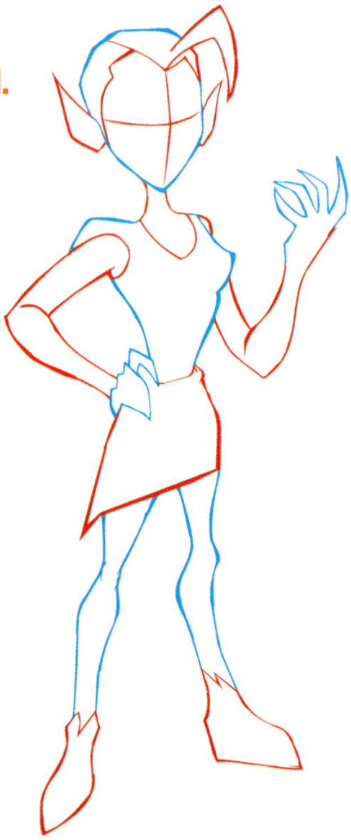

This is ***Kylie*** as an adult. She's much bigger now. Her body and head are now well proportioned. She still has similar features like when she was younger, she's just all grown up.

**Tip:** Coloring your ice character's blue or white will make them look ***cooler!!***

2.

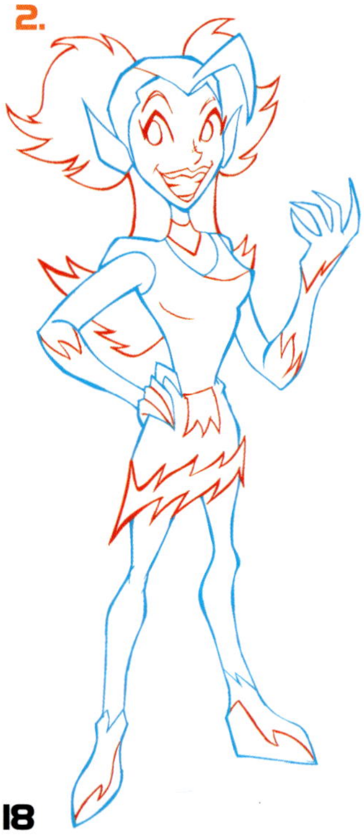

3.

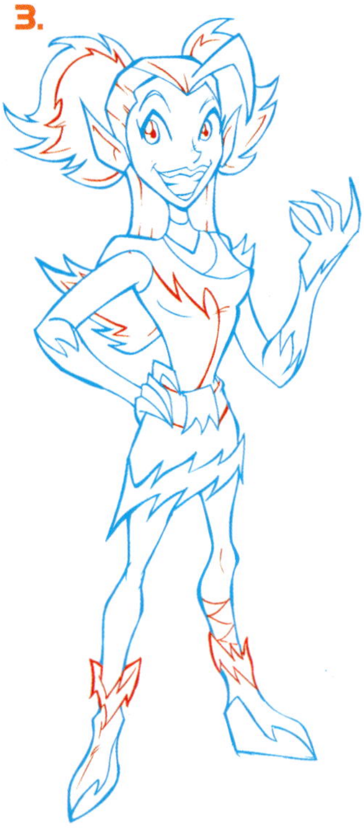

4.

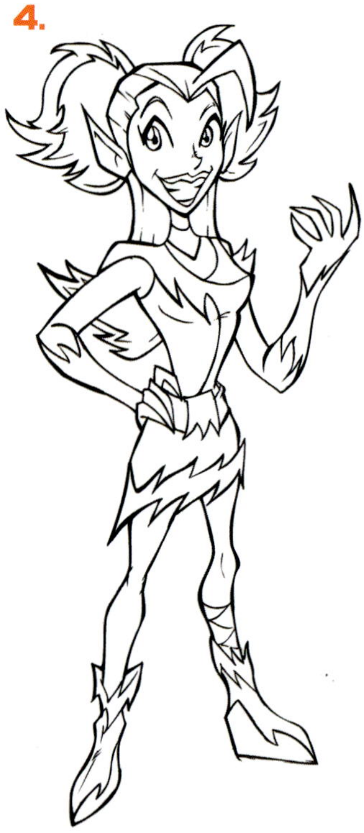

# *Knightly*

1.

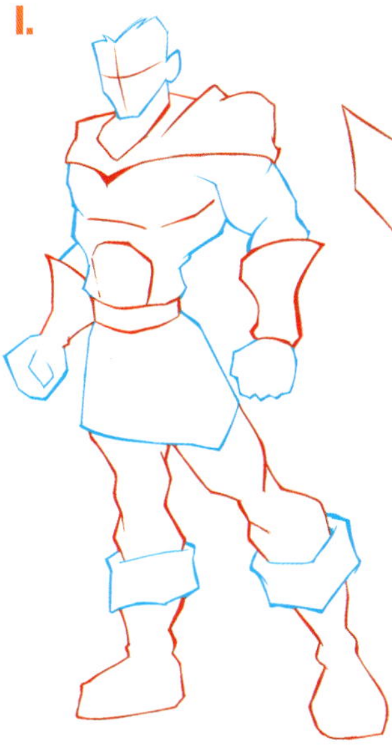

2.

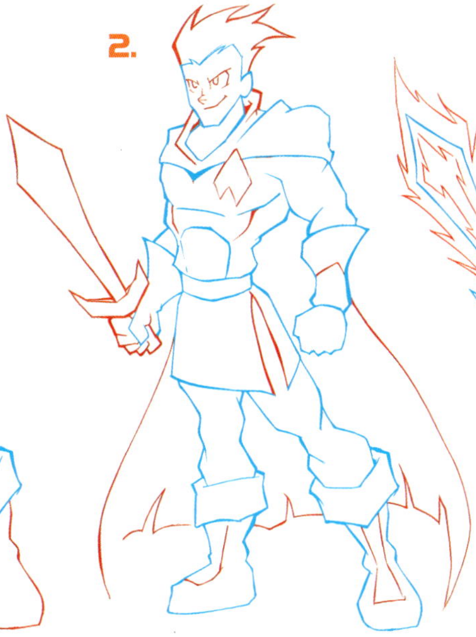

3.

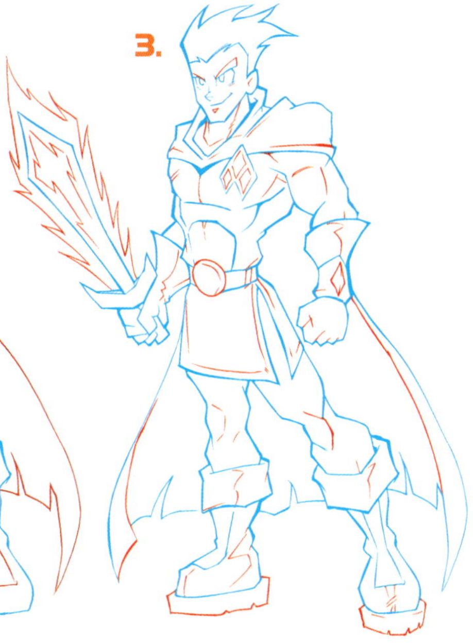

Warrior ***Knightly*** is now an adult. He has finally learned the full power of the Sword of Light. He has become the most powerful knight of his kingdom, following in his fathers footsteps.

4.

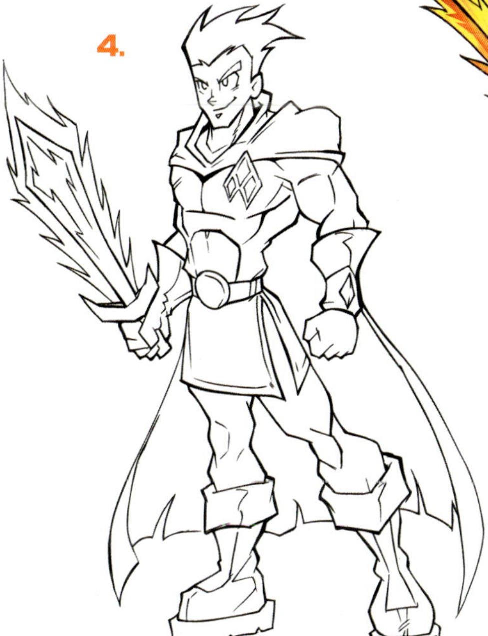

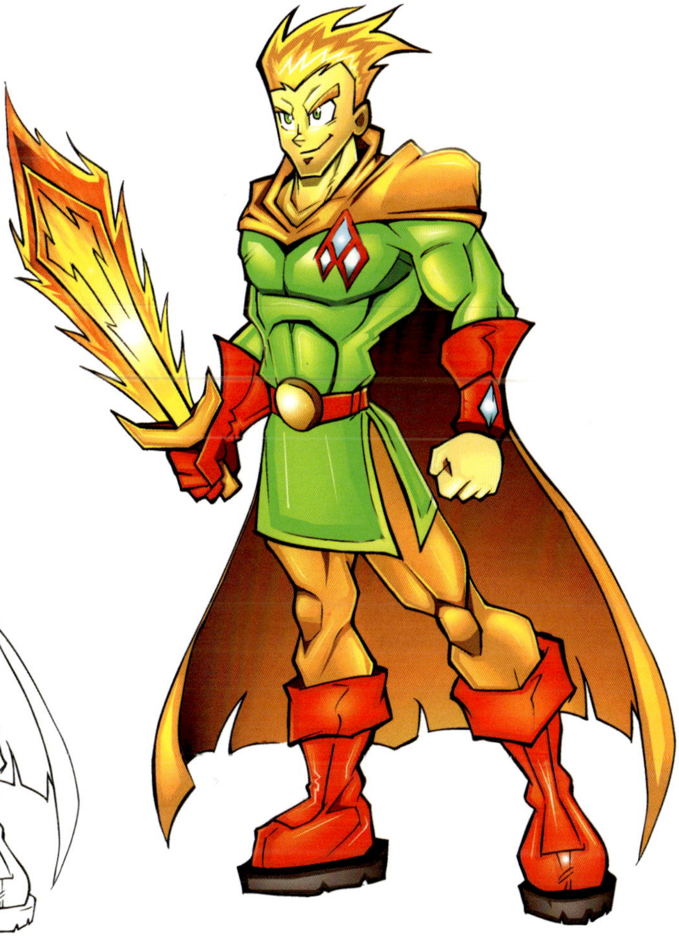

# Cain

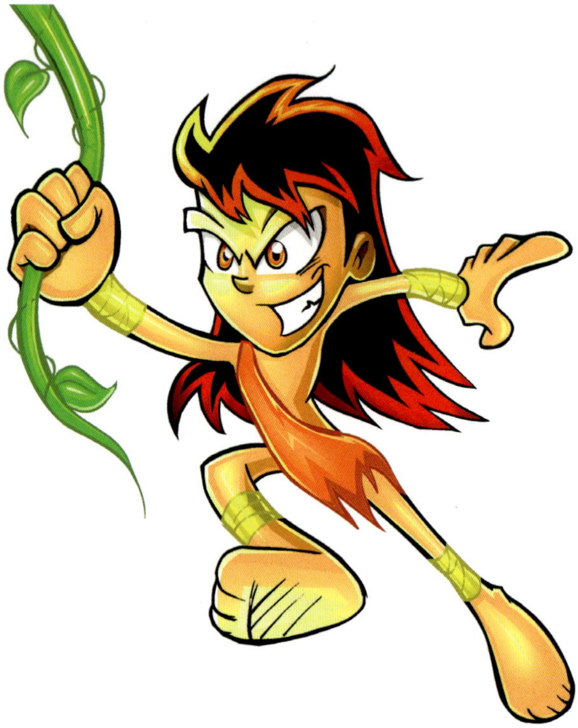

1.

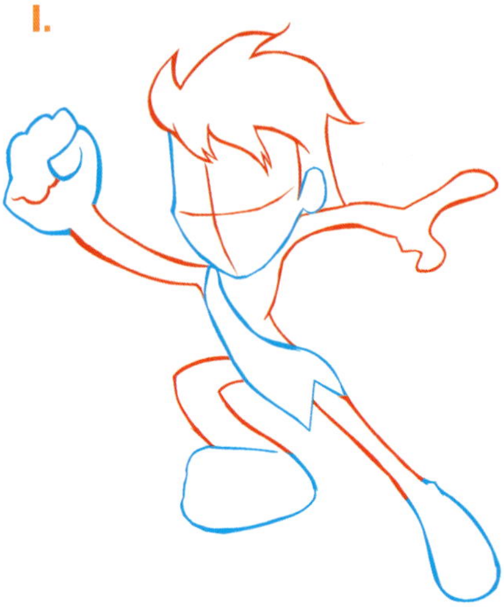

2.

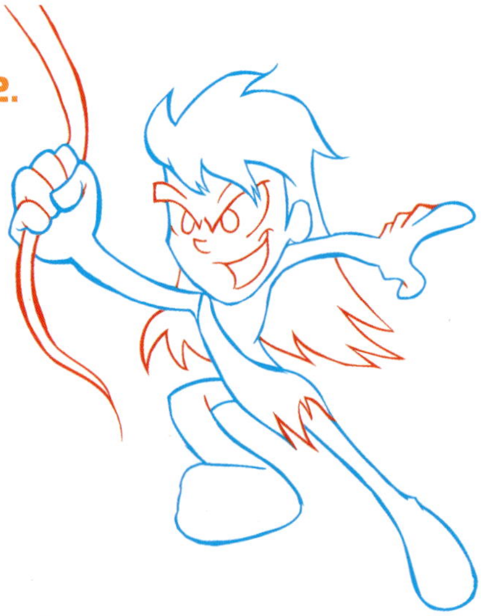

Can you imagine being a jungle character like ***Cain***? Swinging through the jungle on a vine, while dressed in leaves and fur. Jungle characters like Cain and Raven, our Jungle girl on the next page, are very wild. They are fast, strong and take on animal like characteristics like monkeys or apes.

3.

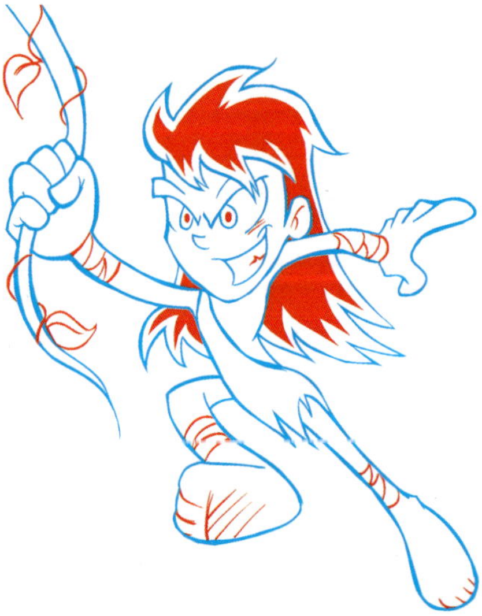

4.

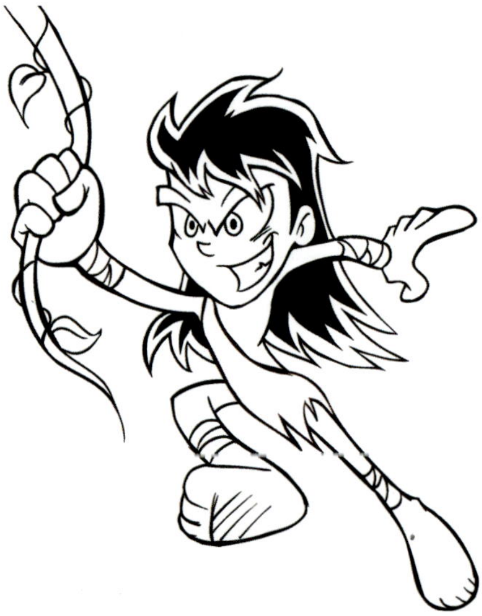

# Raven

1.

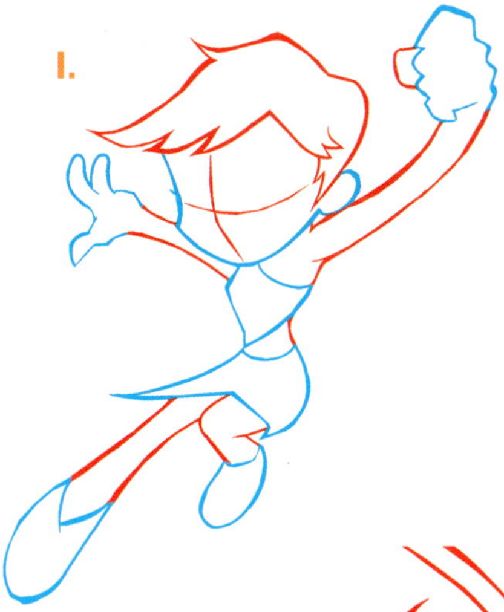

4.

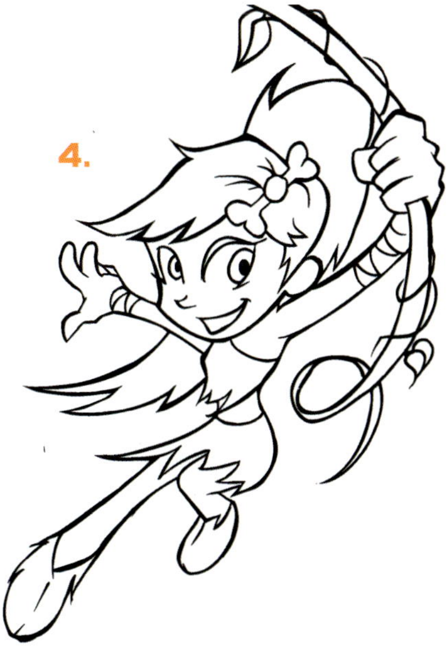

2.

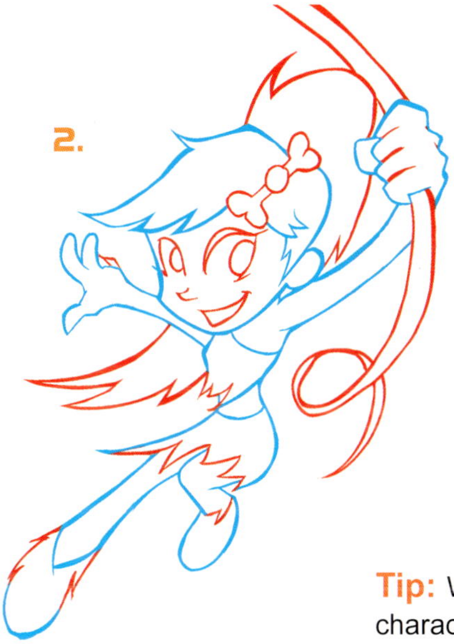

**RAVEN** is a jungle girl character and she is Cain's best friend. Raven is very intelligent and because she has grown up with wild animals, she is able to communicate with them.

Most jungle girl characters are drawn with blonde or dirty blonde hair, but you can draw your character with any color hair!

3.

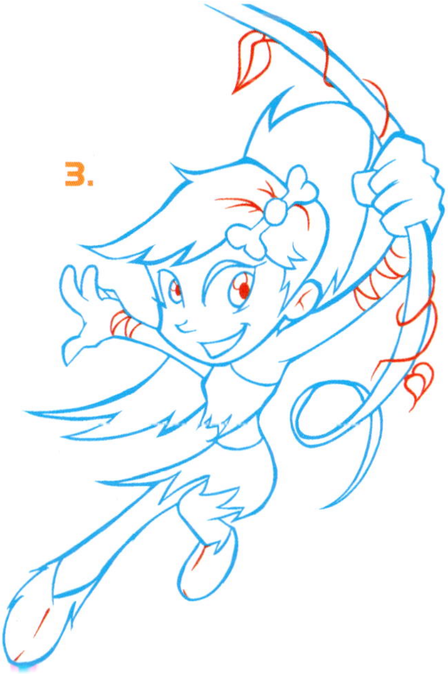

**Tip:** When drawing girl characters draw their eyes slightly bigger then boy characters. Also add eyelashes to the girls, boys are drawn with no eyelashes.

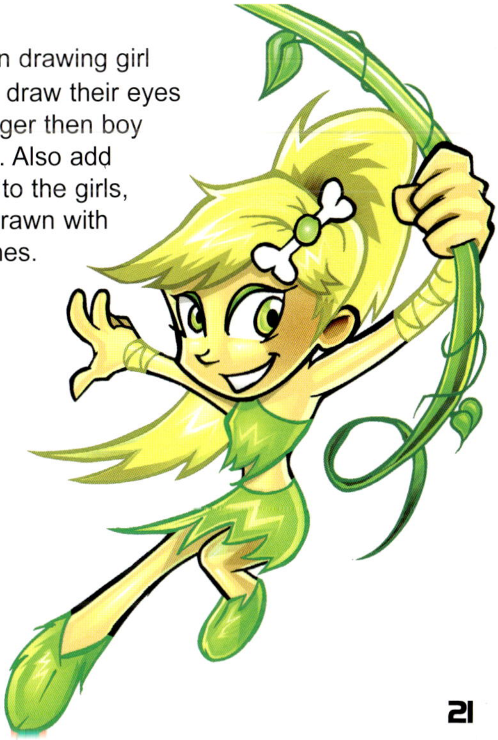

# Little K

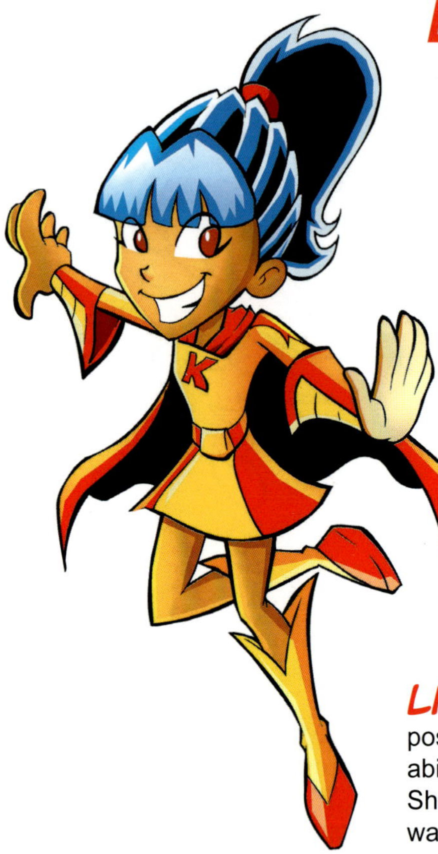

1.

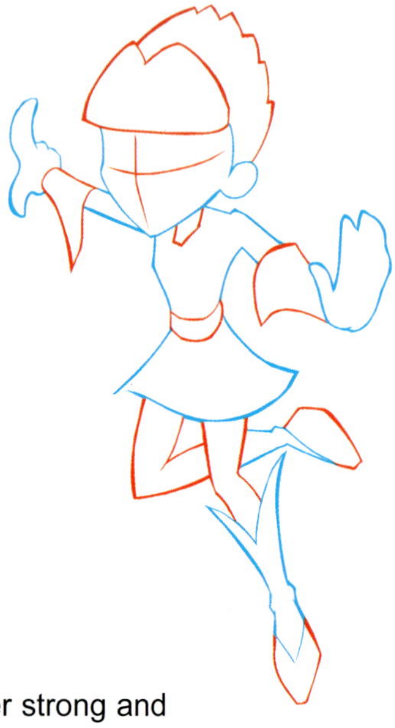

**LITTLE K** is super strong and possesses the power of telekinesis, the ability to move objects with her mind. She developed these powers when she was very young, after a science project gone wrong by her older brother and is now one of the world's most beloved superheroes.

2.

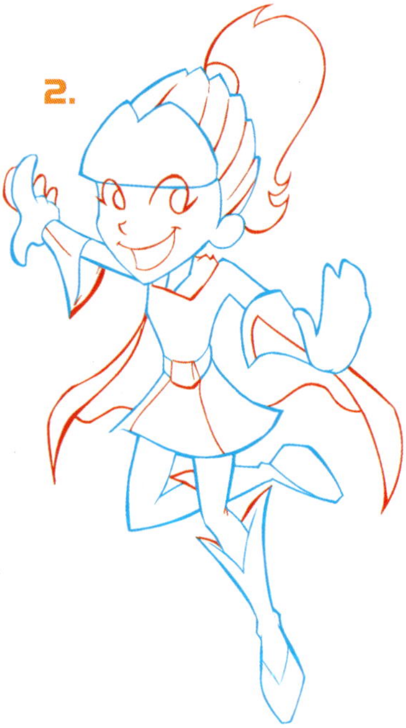

3.

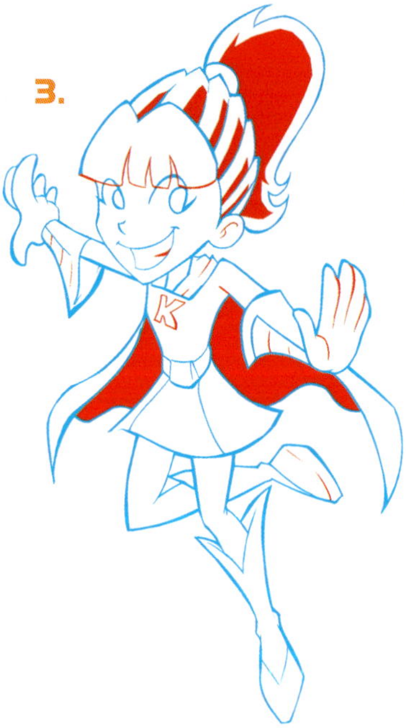

4.

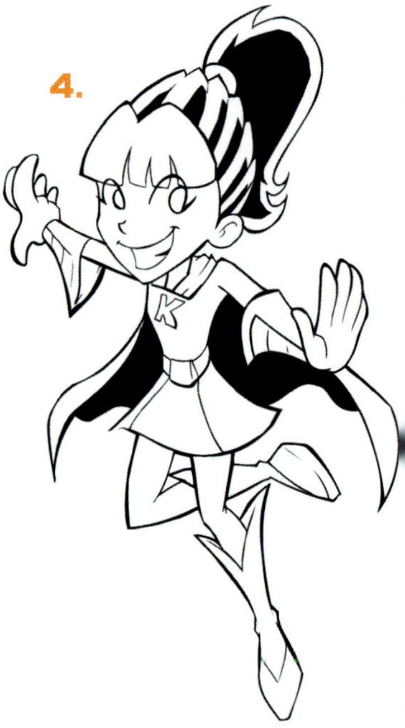

Does your character develop their powers over time or were they born with them?

# Sea Breeze

**SEABREEZE** is a totally cool mermaid, who lives in a castle underwater. She rocks the latest underwater fashions and listens to the hippest music. She also has the ability to communicate with other sea creatures.

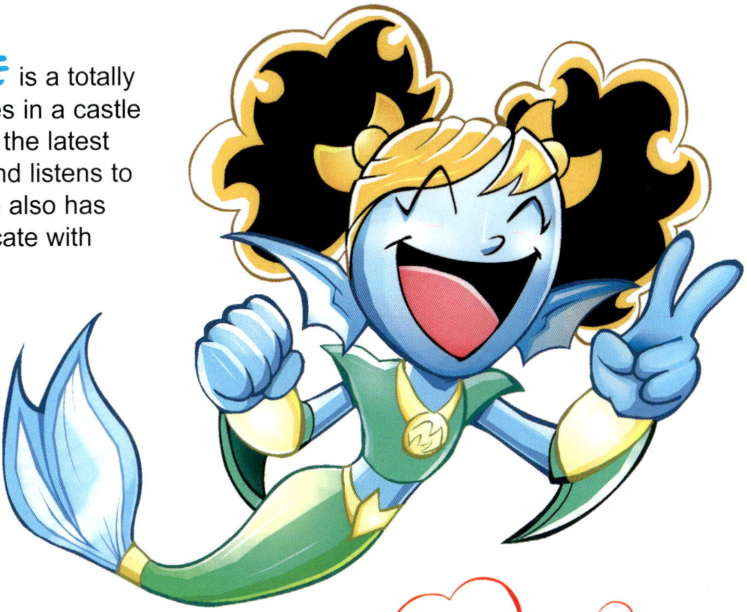

1.

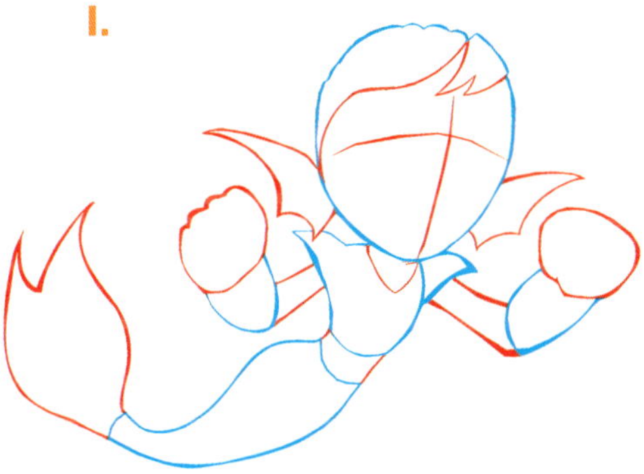

2.

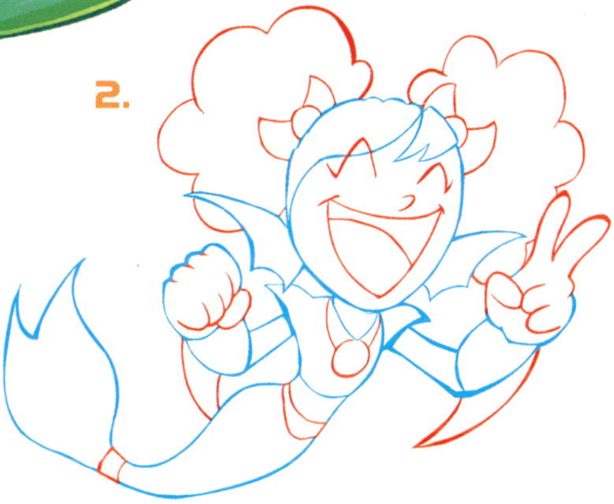

**Tip:** Face expressions really give your character their own personality. Seabreeze is always happy so we draw her with a big smile!

3.

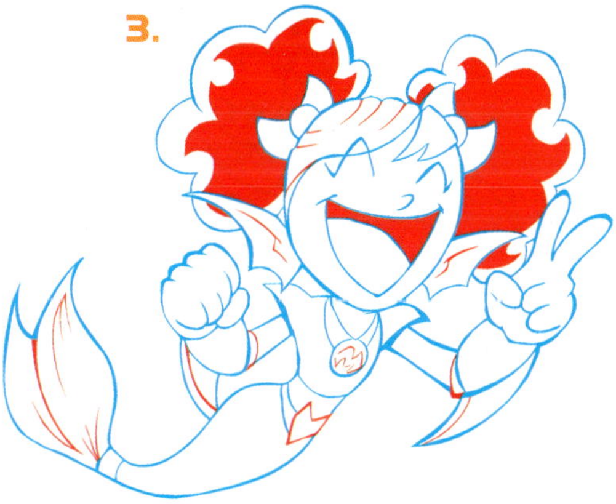

4.

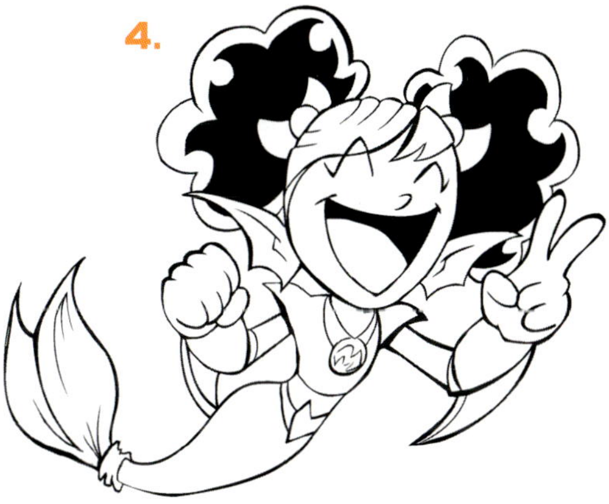

# Draden

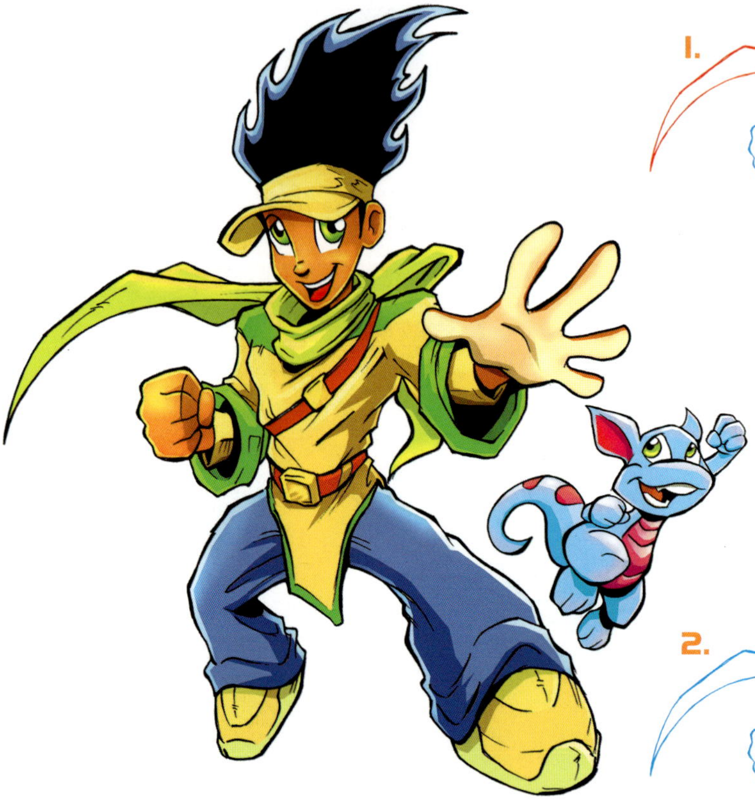

1.

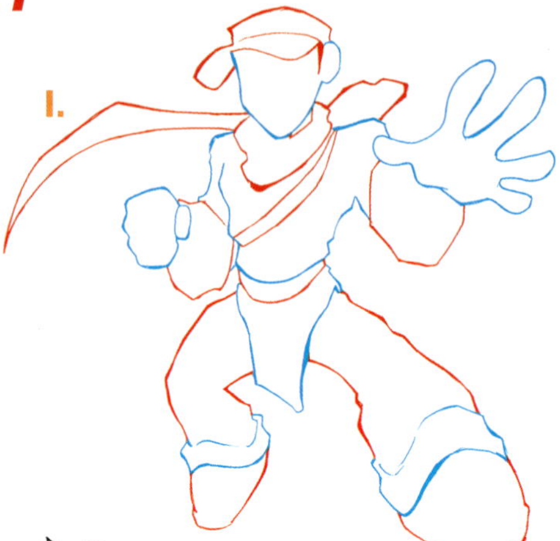

2.

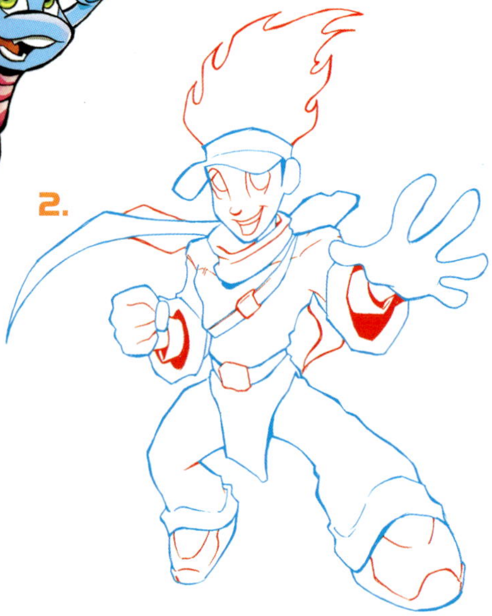

**DRADEN** is a thrill-seeking character who along with his trusted sidekick Nichols, travel the globe searching for hidden treasure. Their adventurous treasure hunts have taken them all over the map!

3.

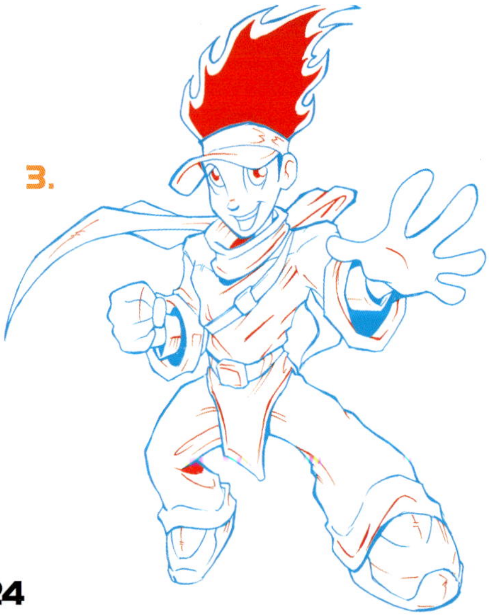

4.

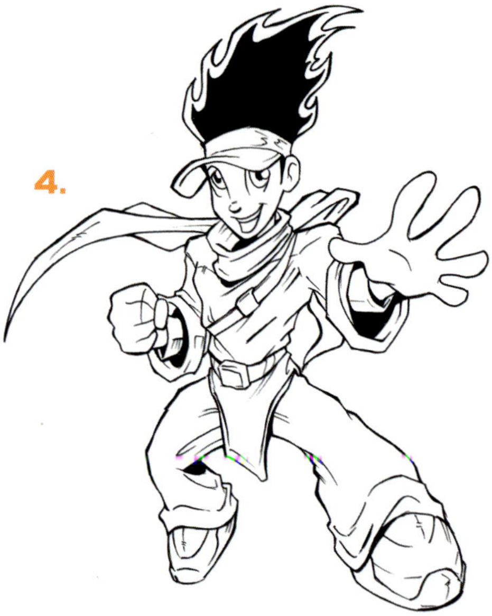

# Monkin

***MONKIN*** What do you get when you take a ten year old boy, a monkey and a super powered suit and mix them all together? You get a character like Monkin!

1.

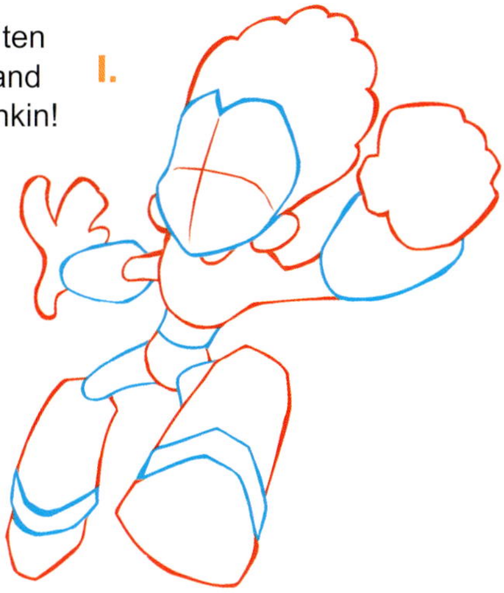

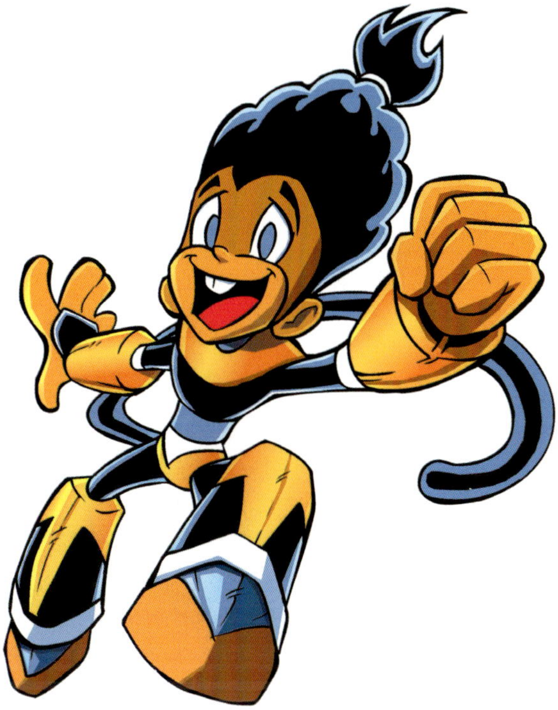

2.

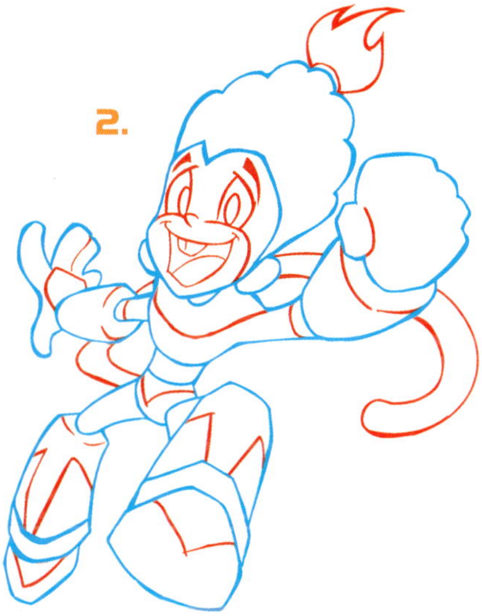

Monkin lives on Planet Banana's. His suit is super strong and allows him to move really fast and breath in space. He can travel the universe from planet to planet at the speed of light! He's still very young and has a lot to learn about his superpowers and what he can do with them.

3.

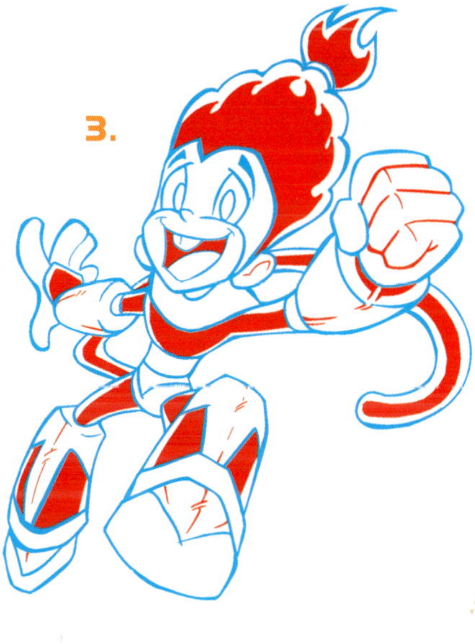

4.

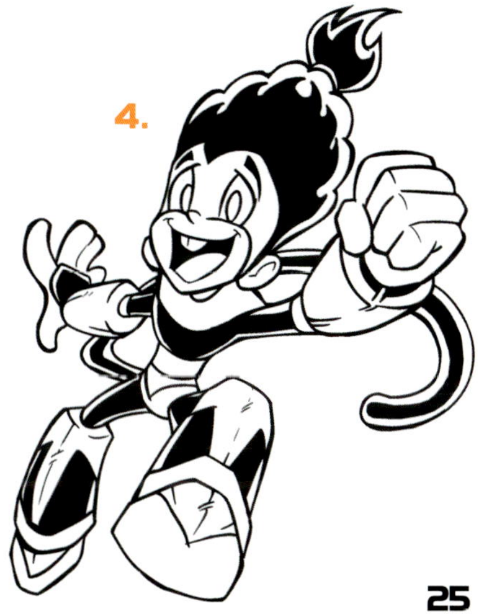

# INFERNO

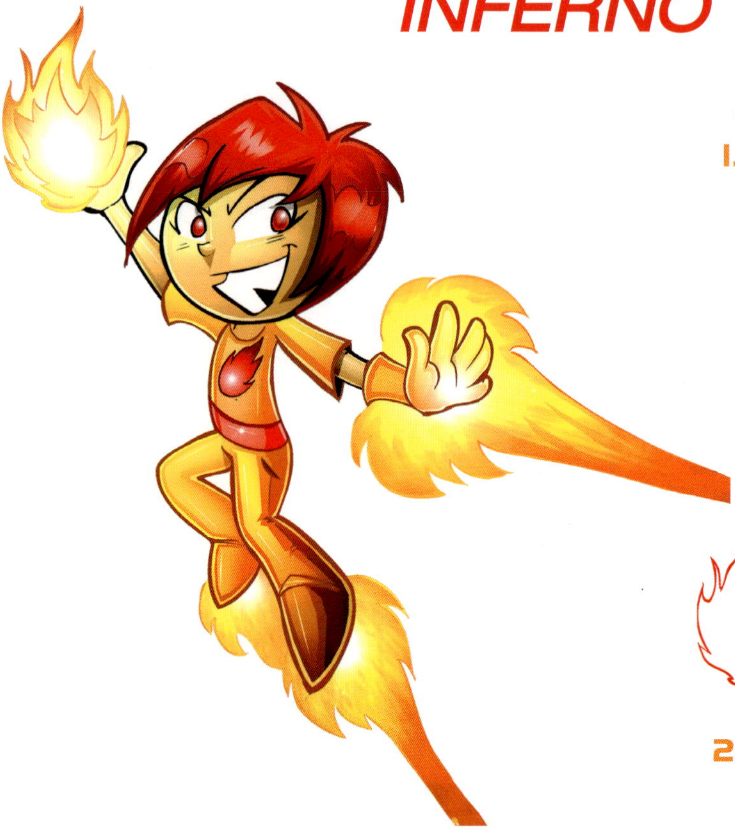

1.

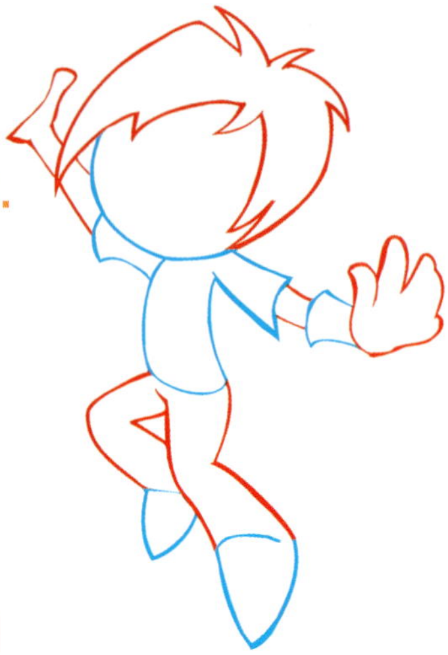

2.

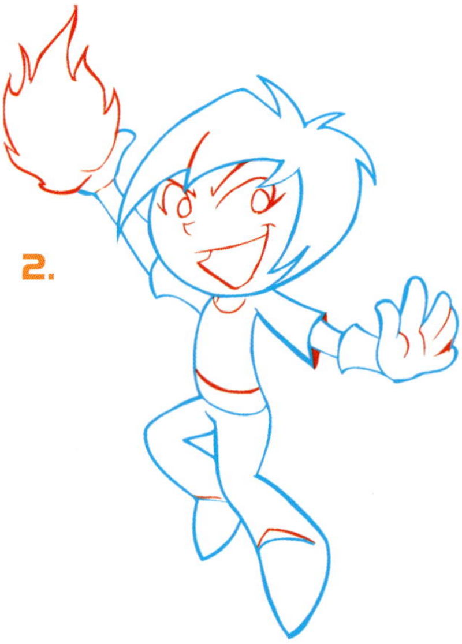

**INFERNO** is a hip and funky character although she's a bit of a hot head! She has the ability to shoot fire balls and she can fly extremely fast.

3.

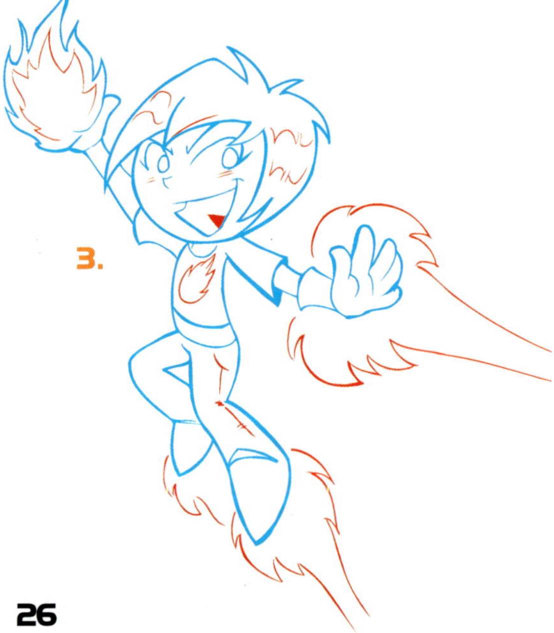

4.

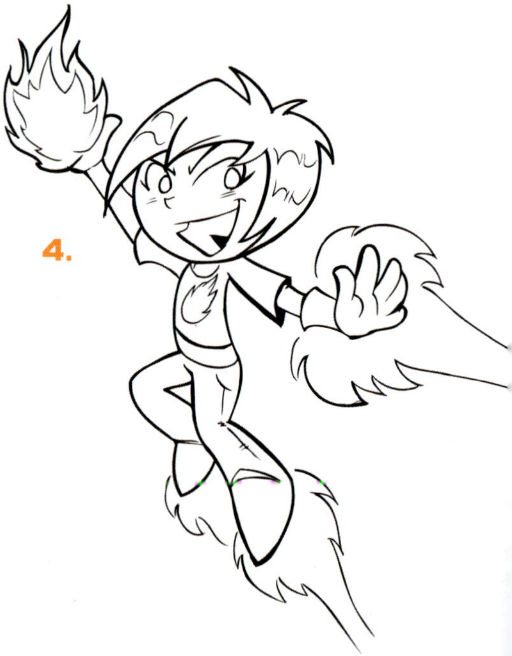

# Wild Storm

1.

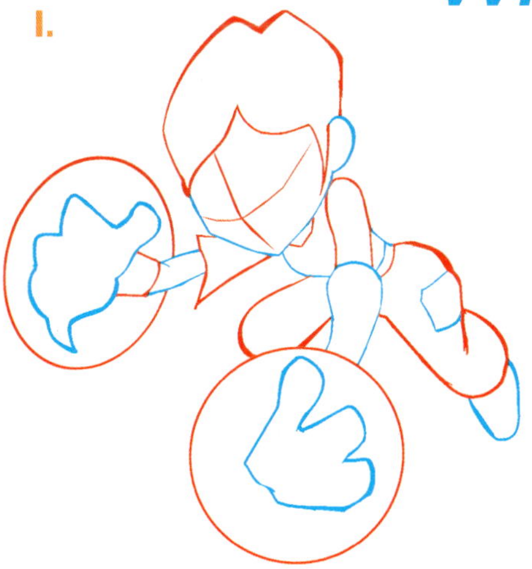

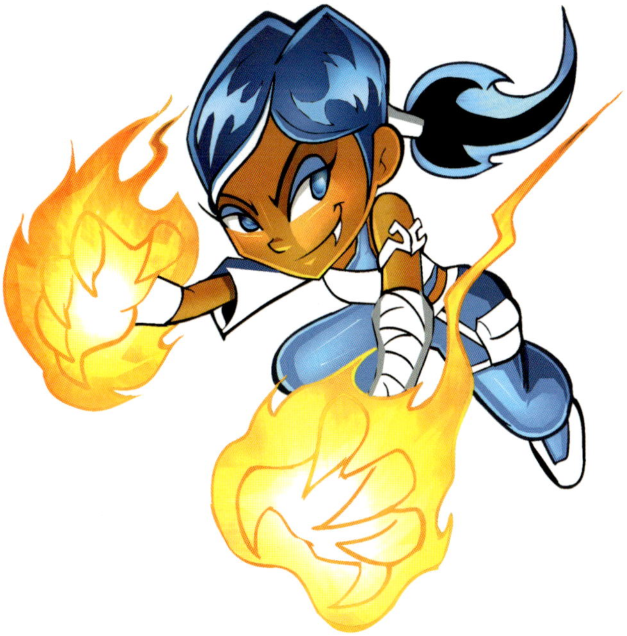

2.

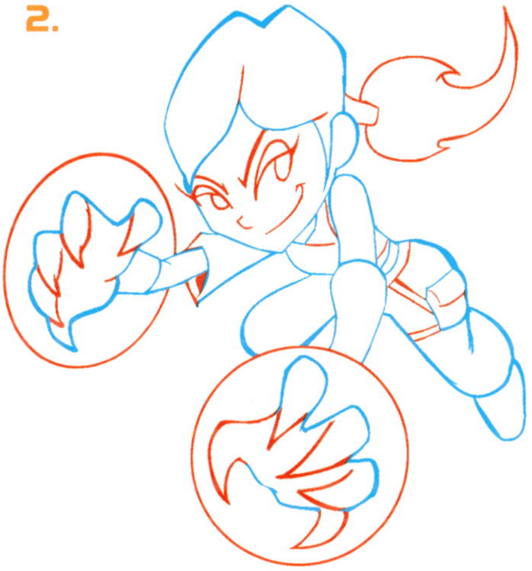

**WILD STORM**, who's real name is Lexi, is a bit of a wild card because no one knows if she's a hero or a villain. She has the power of the elements, earth, fire, water and air. Her favorite power being fire.

3.

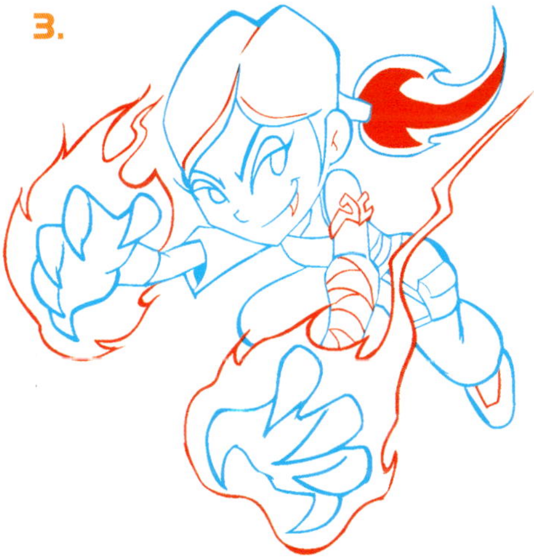

4.

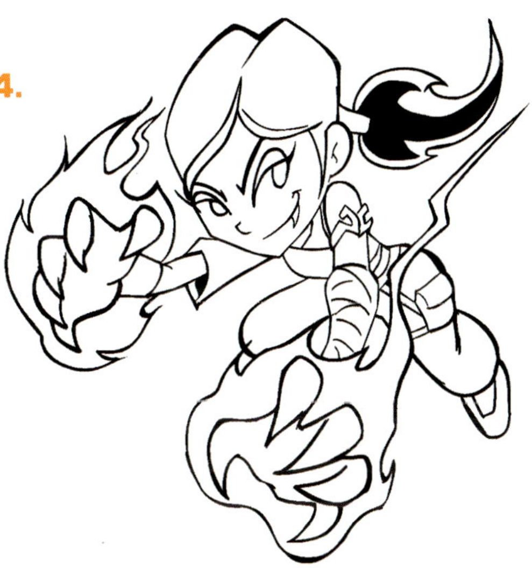

# Maine

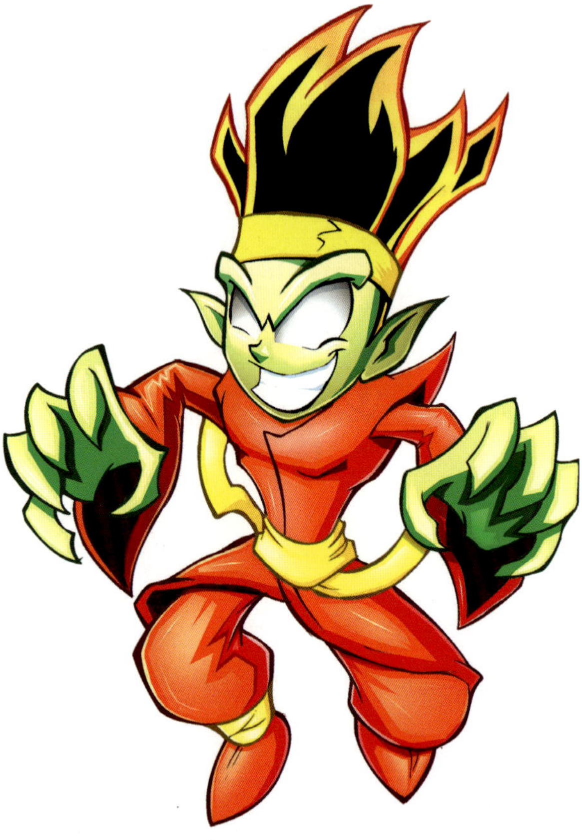

1.

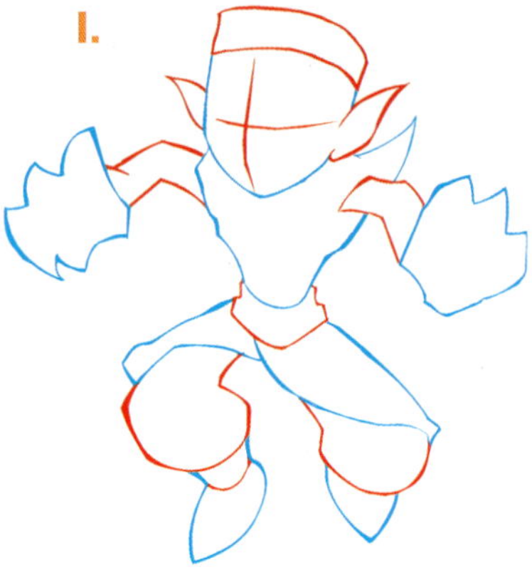

2.

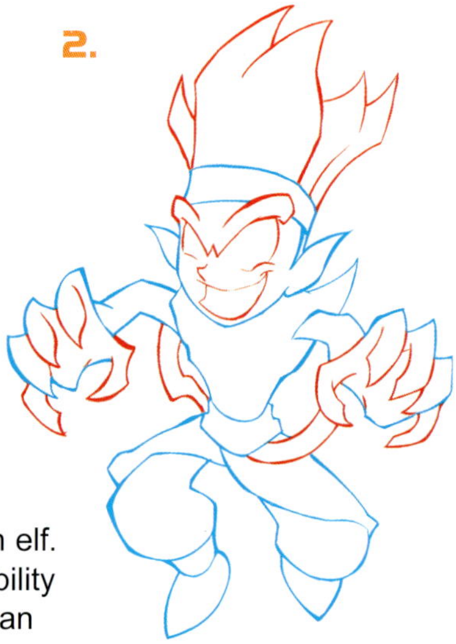

**MAINE** is a ninja character who looks like an elf. He has extraordinary fighting skills, and has the ability to teleport to places he is familiar with or that he can visualize. He can also teleport people or objects.

4.

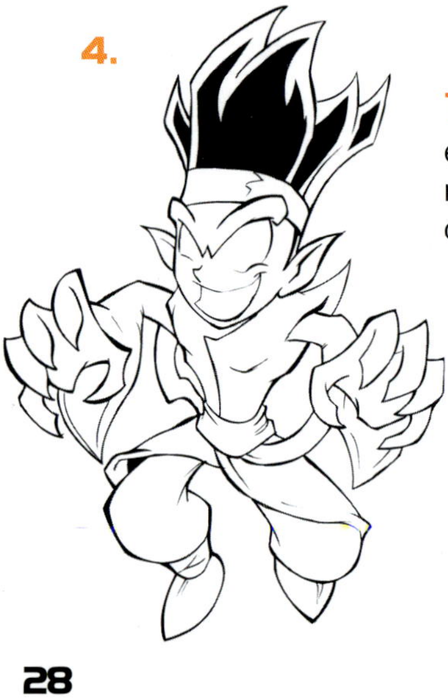

**Tip:** Leaving your characters eyes shaded in one color will make them look more devious or like they are wearing a mask.

3.

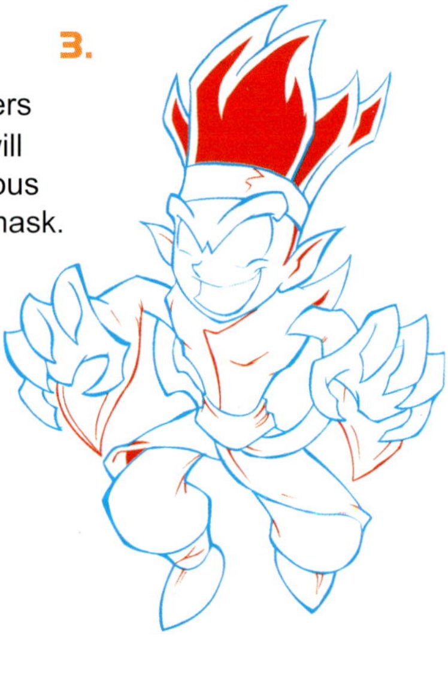

# T-Spike

1.

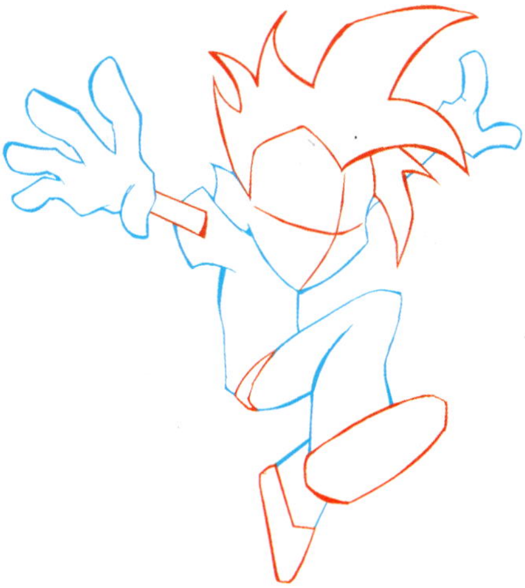

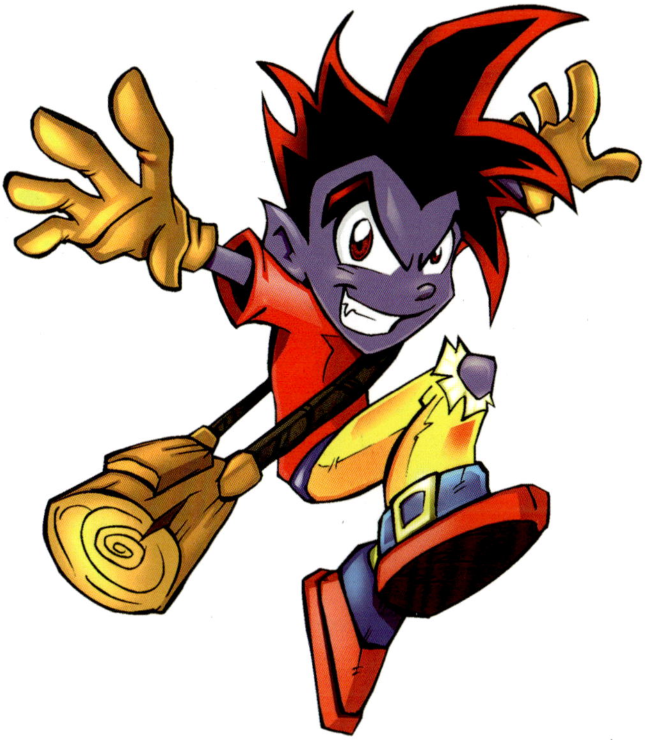

2.

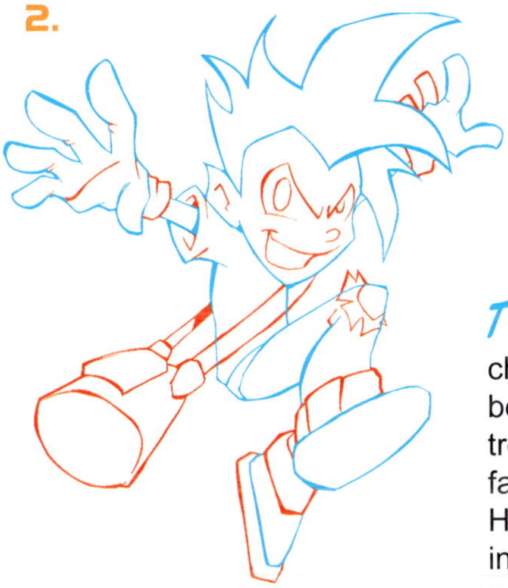

**T-SPIKE** is a wacky, out of control character. He is known in his kingdom for being mischievous and is always getting into trouble. He can leap very high and extremely fast, making him almost impossible to capture. He also possesses the power of shapeshifting into different people and changing his voice to sound like them.

3.

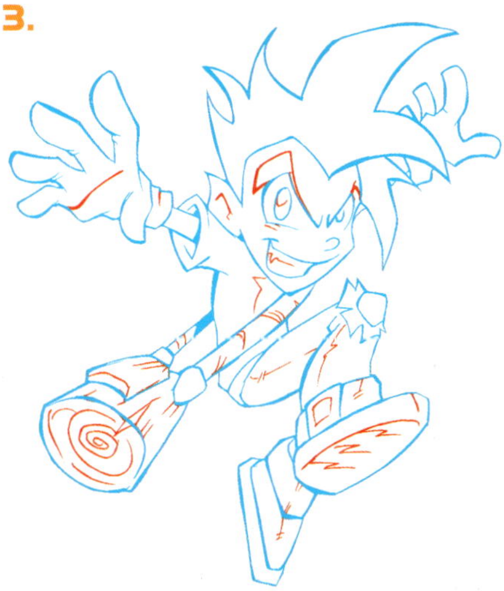

4.

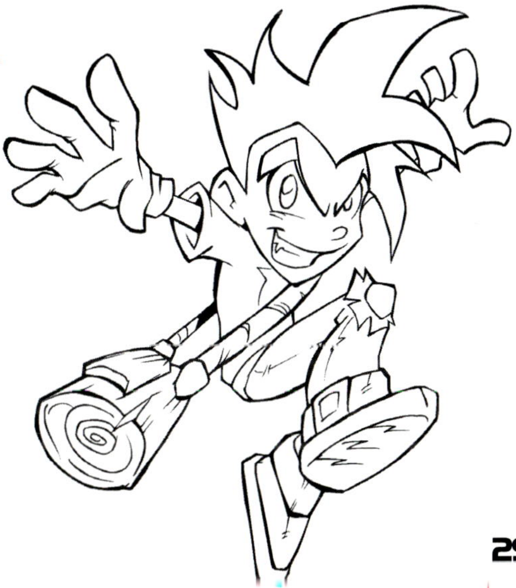

# COLORING

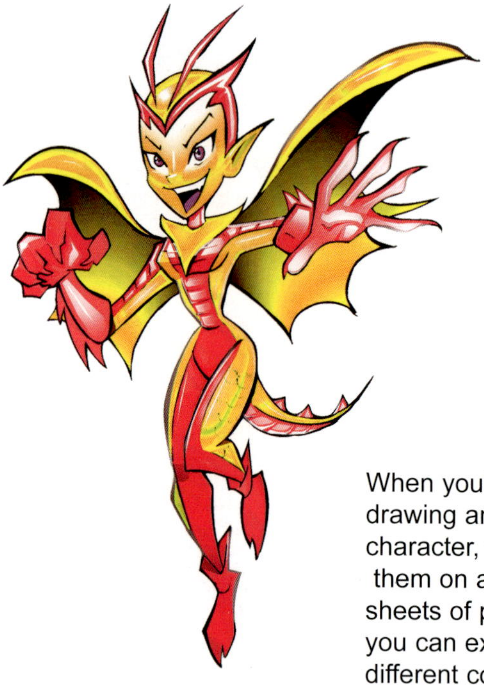

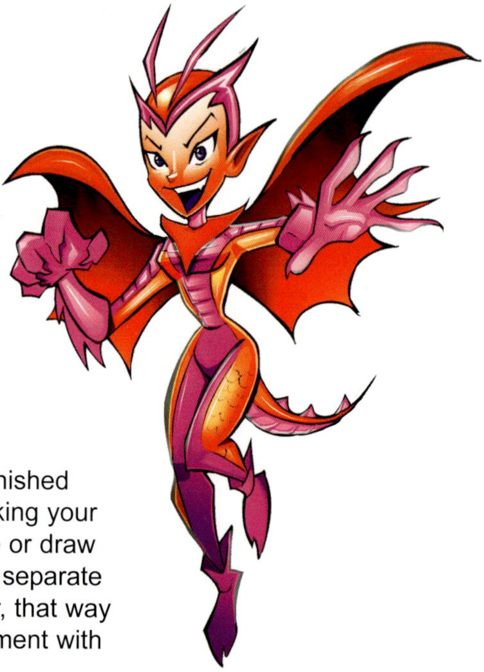

When you've finished drawing and inking your character, trace or draw them on a few separate sheets of paper, that way you can experiment with different colors.

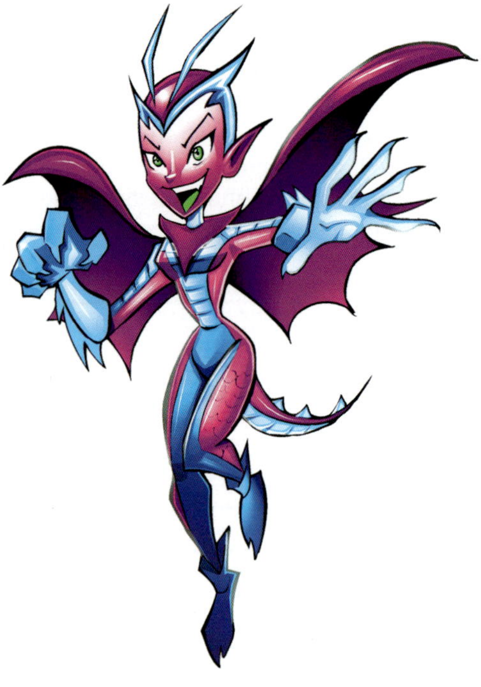

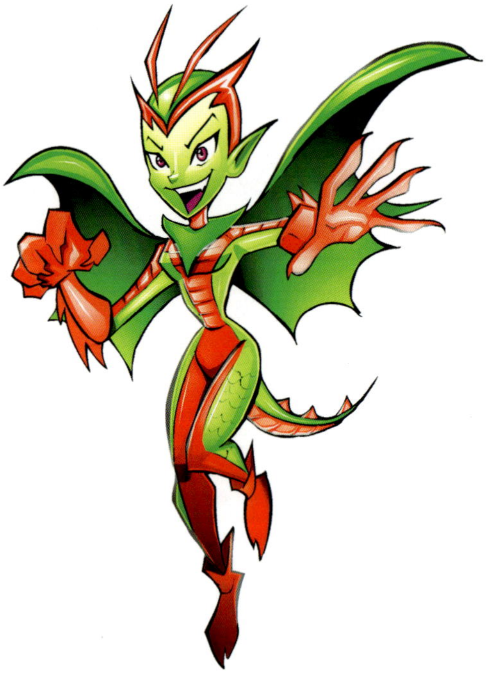

**Tip:** Using bright and sharp colors for your heroes or your good characters will help them stand out more, and dark, dull colors will make your villains or your bad characters look more devious.

# Practice page

Practice by drawing or tracing the figures on this page. In time you will notice you have developed your very own drawing style!

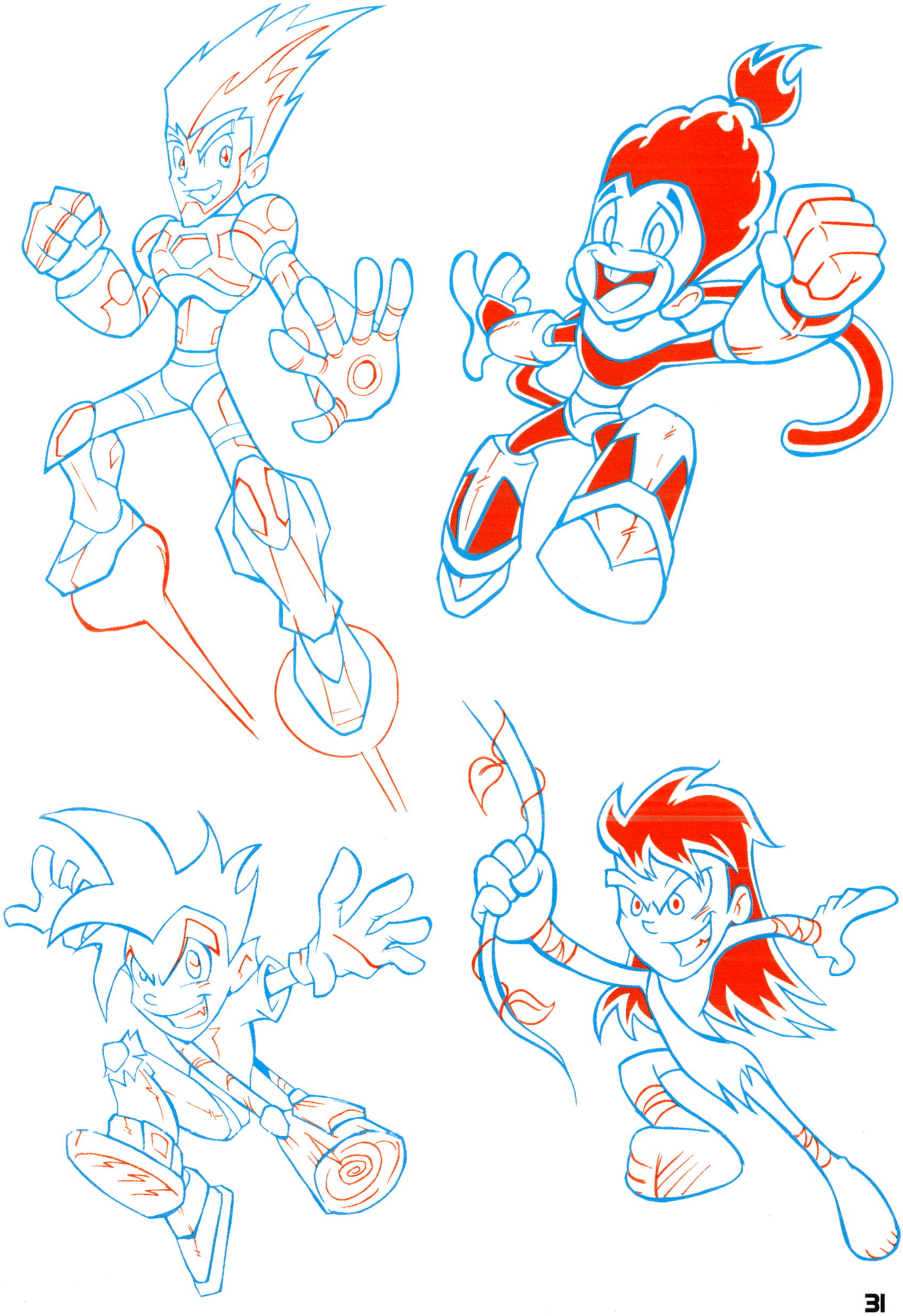

# Practice page

Interested in creating your own comic book? Try our other drawing book series "Create Your Own Comic Book 1" and "Create Your Own Comic Book 2: Heroes and Villains".

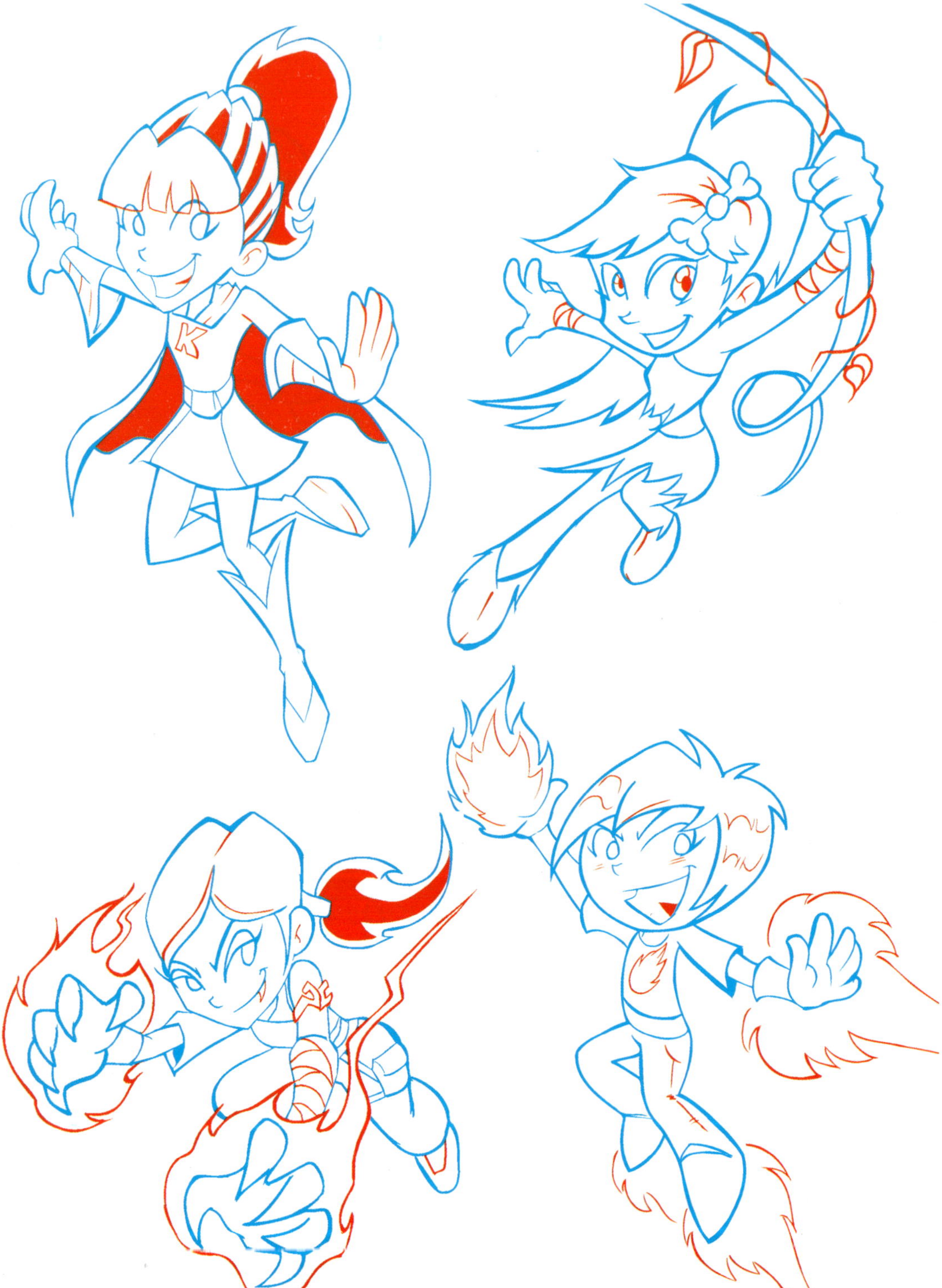



**Tip:** Remember, practicing often will help to improve your drawing skills.